CW00970359

ISBN: 978-1-291-13577-0

LIAM DUNSEATH

Tales of the Unknown Rugger

For my family, friends and extended rugby family.

Chapter 1

It's now 2012 and my twenty-first year of playing this great game. As I sit here in my upper class seat/bed at London Heathrow on the runway waiting to take off on a 10,000 mile round trip, I wonder how did I finally get here, again.

I mean, I'm not talking about this so-called luxury seat on Virgin Atlantic. What I mean is how did I get to being a part of the 2012 USA National Rugby 7s Finals in San Francisco?

A dream I thought would never happen again. I had come back to the UK in 2008 after playing at the USA Nationals, thinking my job was done, that I had achieved something I had never thought possible. Truth be told I came home in 2008 after I had achieved something I had never even thought about or believed could possibly happen. Now, four years later, after many personal developments and highs and lows in my life I was on my way back again. I decided I was too late for the business class lounge, the massage or the beard trim at the airport included when you buy a 1st class ticket...I just wanted to get on board and to get writing.

Another hard journey is in front of me, although at least in comfort for the next few hours this time. All the worries are behind me. I am finally going and ready to play rugby in what will be my last major playing spell. I've waited four years for this. Many personal things have happened in my life. Some have been good and some discouraging. Some things in my life came and went, including jobs, friends and loved ones. Am I prepared physically or mentally? Who knows? I will be able to answer that next week.

But this will determine what I am as a player and what I can offer the team. My role is to cover Doc at scrum half, Ryan at fly half and Dan at centre in case of injuries. I know this because this is what my coach had told me two weeks earlier. I have big shoes to fill and important positions to cover. I will need to be focussed at all times. When I come on I must be ready to make something happen and create chances for our speedsters to capitalise upon by scoring points.

I've played in the USA Finals in California before in 2008, again with my team, Daytona Beach, Florida. We finished 5th in the Nation beating some strong teams that perhaps on another day could have quite easily beaten us. Some of the teams had US Eagle players at the time. The tournament was hosted at Golden Gate Rugby Club on Treasure Island, San Francisco and most teams and critics had written us off but we ended up winning the Plate and finishing 5th place in the nation. I returned to the UK with my head held high. I was still an amateur but it changed the way I saw the world and rugby and most importantly myself and what I could achieve in life through sport.

My journey to Daytona and the rugby team started in 2001. I studied at the University of Salford, Manchester. My best friend, Ben Mosquera, and I decided to go travelling together. I knew Ben from one of the house parties we had on campus at University.

We moved to Daytona in 2001. We flew from the UK and we arrived at Newark airport in New York. We took the subway to Manhattan as we needed to get to Port Authority bus terminal. We drove down to Daytona on a Greyhound coach that took 22 hours, intending to go back to NYC the following week to seek our fortune in the city. I had just $40 in my pocket after I had bought my single bus ticket to Florida. For some reason my student visa electron card was not working at the cash machine. Although we had no work permit we wanted to work casual 'cash-in-hand' jobs, either labouring or in some sort of service industry. Instead of going up to New York, we decided to find work and a place to stay in Daytona. After all it was 80 degrees. There were palm trees and lots of hot American chicks in bikinis. It was a million miles from the wet and cold that

Manchester had to offer at that time of year. Ben was apparently working a dead end job, unsure what to do after finishing his Masters. I didn't really have much interest in my HND course or finishing off the two modules that were uncompleted from the previous year.

There was no Facebook or even Google back in 2001 so I went to yahoo.com and found a local rugby team at an Internet café. I remember there were no smart phones back then. Sure enough I found the Daytona Beach Coconuts and had a chuckle at the name. Would we be playing against the Tampa Bay Tomatoes or the Miami Melons I wondered? The summer of 2001 saw us play 7s in Orlando and St. Petersburg. We would travel with 6 players to the tournament, pick up a couple from other teams and see what happened. Today, over 11 years later, the skill level and organisation is of a much higher standard.

I've been returning to Daytona playing most years ever since.

Chapter 2

In June 2008, Ben and I decided to go back to Florida for a bit of a reunion. I flew standby with a buddy pass costing around half price with Delta Airlines courtesy of one of the rugby guys "Polish Sebastian" or "Seabass" a big American/Polak. He was a good friend who also played rugby. Luckily I was upgraded to business class...what a luxury to start my trip in comfort I thought. Ben was living in Moscow teaching English to rich businessmen's snotty nosed teenagers and that summer he, too, decided to have a break abroad. I played in the Todd Miller Tournament in Orlando and returned to Daytona after a week in LA and Vegas partying with Ben and Matt Meyer. Matt had been an exchange student from Nebraska at our University in the UK. I hadn't seen him since 2000. Our plane had been delayed from Florida and Matt was waiting in LA airport for us. We stayed with Andy Dilsaver, my rugby mate who used to live in Daytona, and we hired a Mustang. Matt drove us to Vegas. In between partying Matt and I would work out in the hotel gym to sweat out all the alcohol. Ben wasn't that keen on training and it was like the good old days for Matt and I when we trained at the University gym. I returned for the USA South Finals hosted by Daytona the week later. It was good to be back. All the old faces were about - Doc, Carlos and some of the newer athletes I had met the previous summer. There was a new guy, Dan Palmer, who was South African. I wasn't too sure at first if he liked me. He hogged the ball and wouldn't pass. He was extremely talented and I spotted this straight away. There was some tension at training between us but we went on to be good friends and have had some great fun together on and off the field over the last four years. I played most games, scoring a bunch of tries. It was very hot and humid so we had to keep hydrating, usually with Gatorade or some kind of sports hydrating fluid. I enjoyed playing very much and played at fly half on a patchy bumpy dry surface. The B-side was looking good too with players like Seabass and Alexi doing well.

The A side was strong with the likes of Rod, Ben, Dan, Isaac and Jordan. We had TJ Lane and "Sugar Shane" as well as Anthony who were great players and athletes, Doc and myself included of course. We beat New Orleans in the final. This qualified us for the National Finals; it was to be three weeks later in California, where the top 16 teams were divided into four pools of four teams for a two-day knock out contest of Rugby 7s. The guys begged me to come as I was now part of something big. I had not even envisaged making the finals and thought I had nothing to lose.

I returned to my job in the UK at Input Media. I showed my boss some of the pictures, all of me of course. I explained about the USA National Finals and its importance to me. He showed some of the pictures to some of the senior directors of the company and they kindly agreed to give me a week's unpaid leave to go.

I would train 19 days out of 21 at home in the UK in between my transatlantic trips and the tournaments. I didn't have a single beer or cigarette. Some days I'd train with Dave, my Royal Marine friend, doing some gymwork and boxing; other days I'd do sprint training in my home town of Epping at the cricket pitch by marking out short routines and exercises. It usually consisted of SAQ drills (speed, agility and quickness), shuttles and endurance stuff. I hadn't done this type of short explosive training before so it was a new learning curve. My friend, Tim, also let me use his gym in Chelsea, London where I'd travel an hour and half to do plyometric leg workouts and super sets. Nothing was going to get in my way. I was focussed every day and every minute. I was constantly replaying scenarios on the pitch in my head during the day while training, at work and in bed. I was excited and felt ready and in extremely good shape.

I again flew standby to Florida from where I'd fly, the next day, with the team to California. However, flying standby again during a busy peak period in August meant the flight was full. With the ticket I had, I was low priority and I would not make the flight. My Dad had driven me to the airport, wished me luck and left. I felt stranded. I was instructed by the airline to wait for the next flight but again swarms of people had a booked reserved ticket and my buddy pass was still low priority. The representatives told me to come back tomorrow or try the later flight out of Heathrow. I was getting very worried and nervous. I randomly bumped into Richard Meagher a friend of mine who was a pilot for BA. He happened to be in the airport. Rich and I used to play up north in Wilmslow. Rather than go all the way home to Essex, we went back to his flat in Clapham, London to review my options. There was a flight out of Edinburgh to Orlando the next day. We booked a BA flight to Edinburgh from London on his laptop and the room for the night and I relaxed at his house for the rest of the afternoon. Worried that I would miss the boys flying out west, my only option was to pay for a flight up to Scotland and a hotel that night to board the quieter flight from Edinburgh to Orlando the next day. If I went back to Gatwick I may have been in the same situation. If I didn't get a flight then that would mean I wouldn't make the flight with the rugby team to California that had been booked and paid for us. I had to fund the flight and hotel to Scotland myself, which was an upset. The only hotel I could get was a luxury Spa and it felt a complete waste of the money better suited to a loving couple for a weekend away rather than just me for a few hours.

I finally boarded the flight and felt relieved. The ship was back on course I thought. I made it over to Orlando, stayed in Daytona that night and the next day we all went back to Orlando to fly out west to California. To get to California meant being on a double legged flight. The flight was hot and very uncomfortable made worse by the annoying behaviour of a guy called Frank Bird Gummey, 12th, better known as "Topper". He decided to crawl over me every five minutes to go to the men's room to drain his winkey. But like any rugby tour we had to have a drink, so I ordered a round of beers for the team costing me and arm and a leg on board. Another passenger kindly bought Dan Palmer and me a beer, too. This random passenger's name was Dean. I've been a Facebook friend with Dean since who's a fun character.

We arrived in San Francisco to a cold and foggy city. Weather-wise, it was very similar to London I thought and probably the rugby conditions were more suited to me. Being from the UK I was used to playing in slightly drizzly and damp conditions. After all this was what most of my playing days in the UK have been like since I originally picked up a ball. We arrived at the airport and took the tram from the airport to the hotel that was located downtown. Some of the other players were arriving and although we would acknowledge the other players and teams, the atmosphere in the lift of the hotel was quite tense. Doc and I went to the gym just to do a light stretch. There was one lad almost galloping on the treadmill sideways. We were pretty impressed he looked in shape but we were concerned why he was doing such an intense work out. Doc advised me not to do anything that might injure myself so I refrained from any strenuous exercise.

That night we had a small social in a local bar. I hadn't had a drink in twenty-two days and was craving a cheeky drinking session. It was like having a little devil dancing on my back. We ended up at a gay bar and at least I can admit to trying to convert a few lesbians with my charm. Needless to say it did not work too well.

The next day, a little jaded after some sightseeing at Fisherman's Wharf, we got down to business on Treasure Island, an old US Military fort where Golden Gate rugby team hosted the 2008 National Finals and we had a team run through.

We practised on the Thursday on a training field covered in goose droppings... no one dropped the ball.

On Friday we checked in at the hotel for the rugby itineraries. I met Al Caravelli, the USA national rugby coach. He heard my accent and asked if I had been brought in as a ringer. I responded by telling him he would find out tomorrow. I cockily winked and walked away. That night we had a team meeting, ate lots of carbohydrates and hydrated. I sent everyone a good luck text message before bed and as soon as my head hit the pillow I was out for the count.

The Saturday morning came around. I was room sharing with Dan Palmer and James Brown otherwise known as Doc. Both are very different people. I've known Doc since 2001, always rolling up his sleeves, with a quaint dopey adorable "Ewok" looking face, always grinning. There is something of a myth in Daytona regarding Doc and his shirts. Some people don't even believe he owns a shirt as he always walk around topless, except at the family doctor's surgery where he works. He would always say phrases like "It's gonna be good!" referring to the night of partying ahead of him or anything really that seemed fun. He was our captain and everyone loved him to bits. He was an animal on the field using his wrestling skills from his college days to his advantage in many game situations, especially in contact, tackling and rucking.

Dan is a South African who has eaten, breathed and slept rugby since birth. He moved over to the USA several years ago. Dan was a hard man; a strong running wizard on the field and a very illusive player. You can tell he has a bit of an animal inside him; a bit barbaric perhaps but a devout Christian. As I said before, when I turned up that summer there seemed to be some tension, perhaps me as a Brit and him as a Saffa. I didn't like his arrogance on the field. And he didn't like me either. Now we are top friends and have a good heart to heart once in a while. He has been a very inspiring player. He has admitted since that, yes he didn't like me either at the beginning so it shows how the tide was now turned.

Our first game at Nationals was against Sciotto Valley, a team from Ohio. Previously I had made a joke that at 100:1 what are the chances of me scoring the first try? It was an early start and it may have been the first game of the tournament. The place seemed a bit dead and hadn't got too much life at that time of the day. I was fresh though and ready for it. I should have taken that bet, as it was yours truly with a fake dummy scissors that scored under the posts from inside their 22-meter. I had a smile from ear to ear. However, this would prove to be my only try of the tournament. Belmont Shore RFC creamed us with the US Eagle Dellan Stanford as their playmaker. I remember Gillanwater another US player defended against me with ease and I had to pull out of many tackle situations to keep the ball alive, as I was not going to beat him on the outside. Our final game in the pool was against Austin Elite, Texas. It was also a tough one. I made some massive hits and was extremely pumped. I was gunned down after a 60 m run only to off load to Mark Eichner who went over to score. You can hear on the video tape the crowd saying, "Oh, I think he ran out of steam, he didn't have the legs". I wasn't too bothered really as we scored some points that got us to the quarterfinals.

We had made the quarterfinals. I played a few minutes at the end against Aspen the following day where our defence struggled from the start and the game was lost in the first half. Mike Pelefau the US Eagle was playing in that game. He went on to make most valuable player of the tournament or MVP as they call it. We made the Plate semi finals against Maryland Exiles where it was do or die. I tackled my heart out, a rarity, constantly waiting for the whistle to go in a tense game. We smashed them and this was probably my best game coming off the field ten feet tall. We were now in the Plate final.

I played no part against Chicago Lions in the final but we had won and it didn't matter. We were now USA 2008 Rugby 7s Plate Champions. I was the first player to christen the Plate and drank Guinness out of it. We had some team photos and all of us were grinning from ear to ear. Some of the other teams had written us off and we had shocked them and the USA rugby community. In the words of Brian Richardson when I interviewed him later back at Orlando airport, he said, "It was that little club that could!"

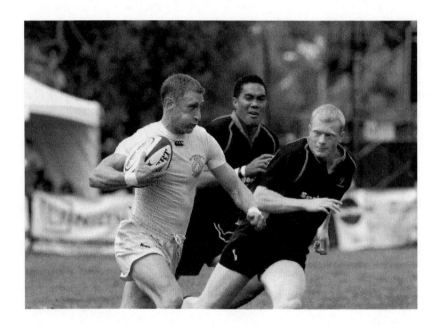

I was shattered from making those two trips over to the USA (the first one being the South Finals in Florida and the 2nd being the National Finals in California) and juggling the flights, costs and dates etc. as well as organising my unpaid leave. I had a bit of a go at a few of the players and snapped at a small thing regarding some off the field incidents that will remain unknown. I was simply tired. I had trained so hard and learnt things about running and myself that I never knew. It was tough for me to not have played in the final or in the game against Aspen but it was Brian's decision. I remember seeing some of the players and their defence was non existent as if they were half asleep looking around at each other mindlessly as if to say they were confused as to what was going on. I could only watch from the sideline and it's easy to be a critic when you are not in the heat of the moment playing and gasping for air.

I remember returning extremely proud to the UK. I was showing the airhostesses my programme in which I was pictured in. I had a new spring in my step although I didn't want to touch a rugby ball for at least a month. I was tired physically and mentally. I had plotted in my head and envisaged game situations all summer. This happened every day and every second. I would think about rugby, the team and how I would play. Now I could let go. I felt I was free that I had conquered a massive landmark in rugby and in my life. This was one of my proudest times in rugby and I was sure to come back home and brag about our achievements to anyone that would listen.

Throughout the trip I would make little videos on my digital camera. The boys weren't too sure why and what I was doing. Once I edited it all together added some music and some graphics from work and a voiceover they all seemed to like it. I posted it on Facebook as a momento for everyone, friends and family included.

Figure 1 Daytona win 5th place at the USA National 7s finals 2008

Chapter 3

So, I had returned to the UK...and now what? Well, I joined Barking Rugby Club and moved to Battersea, London in December 2008. However, I only managed second team and, due to working for the sports television network each weekend, I could never play. It was a fairly good set up. Kevin Sorrel from Saracens, who was in my sister's year at school, coached the backs. He was in the back end of his playing days and I guess he was considering going into coaching. The pre-season fitness was good and I was in shape from the summer. But it was fair to say for that season and the start of the next due to working weekends covering televised sport, my time at Barking faded.

By the spring of 2009 I had now moved to Battersea and lived with a Iranian guy called Hadi who had posted an advert online for a room in his flat. We became good friends and wingmen and like me he was very competitive. We would train in the gym and sometimes he would come and sprint with me in the park although I'd kick his ass in any type of sprint. He wasn't used to this style of training but he knuckled down and finished the job well. Anthony Muniz from Daytona flew over to visit me and stay. I showed him what the wild side of London has to offer and he took a liking to many of the English girls. We also trained in Battersea Park. He claimed that I only beat him as I was wearing rugby boots and his trainers had no grip on the moist grass. No one likes excuses I thought. I was now quicker than him and I had better acceleration and he knew it!

In the summer of 2009, I returned to Florida even after being threatened with redundancy in my job. Our main client was an Irish sports network called Setanta who were forced into liquidation. The production company that took care of their services, and I worked for, was also in jeopardy. I thought if I lost my job I would be broke, but then I thought what happens if I keep my job and don't take the opportunity to go and play? Perhaps I will do better playing than I had done the year before.

I spoke to Chris my boss and he said to go over and play, regardless.

So I would go to Battersea Park around the corner to where I lived to run and to the Fitness First gym in Clapham Junction. Sometimes I'd trained with my good housemate, Hadi. From February to June 2009 I had been working hard on sprinting technique, anaerobic and sheer, hard, horrible conditioning. I had downloaded the official USA conditioning, off season, speed and gym routine/workout and would take a few sessions a week to blast out 50/100 sprints covering from 5m, 10m, 20m, 50m, 100m with the least amount of recovery time. I was in good nick probably better than the year before and I also had a lot of confidence. I started going to the running track too, in Battersea Park, where I would go on Friday nights in the spring and do six-eight x 400m sprints to build a platform. I had met Ben Wilson at the Clapham Common touch rugby group and he was training 400m sessions so he invited a few of us along regardless of how fast we were.

I would train on my lunch breaks from work in the local park of Ravenscroft, London. Time was ticking. This year though, the South Finals happened to be up in Georgia, a long five to six hour drive from Daytona.

So I flew over stateside again. I stayed in Daytona again with Doc and Pat and then we all travelled up to Georgia. It would be just a seven-day trip this time. I had been over in the spring of 2009. As I had played in one of the regular 15's season games, I was CIPP registered as a Daytona player and would qualify automatically for 7s and the South Finals.

The drive up was long and hot. The tournament was based at a military fort a few hours away from Atlanta. It didn't go well. Disaster struck. Player after player seemed to get injured. Doc unfortunately suffered a concussion and Scott picked up
had hosted the South Finals. We had local support and we went

on to win the tournament. The trip up this year to the military base was a disaster and we left with nothing. We left with just the memories from the previous year and the ones of this trip's failure; but that is rugby. Injuries will make or break a team. It was just one of those things. People went their different ways home; some straight to the airport in Atlanta. Jordan's brother who was down supporting went back to Pittsburgh and Dan's cousin, Bruce, flew straight home back to Cape Town. It was a great shame as everyone had been so excited and seemed ready. Sometimes it's just not your time to shine. Sometimes it just doesn't happen despite how much you want it. Being there was the easy part. Winning was the tough part. There always needs to be a loser. It's cruel but that's the nature of the game. That's sport and that's rugby. I knew this as well as everyone else.

After 2009 I didn't fly back to Florida for a holiday or for rugby.

A few months later that summer, I met a lovely girl named Kirsty who, within a few months, became my girlfriend. She lived in a flat in Putney, London with another girl and her boyfriend.

My boss, Chris Payne had been playing for Wimbledon RFC for some years and suggested I went down to play. I knew a few of the lads from the rugby netball game Chris had also introduced me to that summer. Training was OK but it was a long way to get to and a pain in the arse to get back home from, even if I got a lift with Danny Craven and Chris Lewis. I played a few games and had a lot of fun in the second team but the selection process was weird. They would post the team on the Internet. I was unaware of this and I hadn't realised. Consequently, I didn't turn up the following week as no one told me so I went out on the lash the Friday night and never made the game. To be honest I wanted to play a higher standard of rugby than at Wimbledon RFC and perhaps I thought I was better than I actually was.

So, after a few months, I joined Rosslyn Park RFC, who at the time were in National Division One, two leagues below the Premiership. I was slightly out of my depth again but around in a professional environment, coached by Stuart Abbot, an ex-England player and World Cup winner of 2003, meant that I was attentive and trained hard on training days and in the gym.

Rosslyn Park RFC was near to Kristy's flat and I would love coming home aching and tired to some of her lovely dinners, some lemon and honey, a hot bath and a cuddle with her.

Coaching at the club consisted of video analysis of the First team's previous Saturday game. There would be a Q&A and a chance for the players to give their opinions. Sometimes a member of the IRB referees committee would come and talk to us about the new laws being implemented, to teach and guide players. We would warm up professionally as a squad. No one ever played touch rugby. I wasn't sure if the First team was too cool or if it was just frowned upon as an amateur warm up. Dynamic and static stretching took place, followed by team warm ups using special awareness drills. We would play a netball style game, passing in all directions to help our bodies warm up but also to improve our special awareness. We might have a rucking drill or 8-10 minutes of painful short shuttle runs and fitness. Then, the backs and forwards would split. It was good club level rugby and I enjoyed the set up. It was weird though to walk into a changing room and sometimes a few players would not even acknowledge you or say hello. Some of the players were on loan from London Irish, London Wasps or Harlequins. I guess they weren't there to make friends unless they already knew you. I would have to earn respect on the field. There was no drinking after training or socialising. There was a team of four physios and it was great to grab some free treatment however long you had to wait. You could book in advance though. I had some calf strains from the track I assumed, horrible knots that meant my shins would hurt. The lady massaged them out. One time I had acupuncture, a privilege for some rugby players and clubs. I played a bunch of good games for the second team at Full Back against an Army regiment consisting of Fijian soldiers where I scored on my debut. Apparently they had all come back from Afghanistan and had lost a lot of men. It was a cold night and knowing that they didn't like the cold I thought we might have the upper hand. I ended up getting snotted by one of the Fijians who played in the army regiment. I'm sure it was a late challenge. I was meandering around the pitch not sure in which direction I was going, what the score was or what I was actually supposed to be doing. Luckily, Rob Boultwood, the 2nd team manager sorted me out and when I came through Kirsty came down to pick me up in her pyjamas, worried sick, as she had received a phone call saying I was in cuckoo land. I also played against Esher which proved to be a horrible dogfight as well as playing against a few other teams around southwest London. It was a shame I would suffer a heart palpitation against Richmond, my old club, where I wanted to stick one on my old teammates from 2006-7. Stuart Abbot was in charge that day and my heartbeat became erratic which resulted in me coming off, (just as it had done in 2002.) Only this time I knew to caress the Carotid artery. This sends a signal to the brain to slow down the amount of heartbeats. After it went back to normal resting level he refused all game to let me back on and play. I was gutted after training hard all week and having my girlfriend come down to watch me play. I played one game where Kirsty and John the builder, my mate, would come to watch at the home ground. Apparently I didn't make much contact or tackling keeping my kit nice and clean. John would heckle "Oiii Dunners Persil Whites...keep ya whites white" My sister brought my niece Leah once and apparently she thought everyone was me and extremely fast "Uncle fast...uncle fast" she told her mother.

I didn't play much the rest of the season due to work commitments for I was now working for a radio transmission centre that engineered worldwide radio channels. I would work seven days on and seven days off. The first week I would work 7am-7 pm then the following week would be 7 pm-7 am. On this shift, I had no life as I slept all day to recover from the long hours overnight and it would mean a week of no rugby.

In the April of 2010, I played rugby league for Hainault Bulldogs. I had done well two years previously setting me up for my fitness before my trips to the USA that summer, returning as a National and South finals winner. My first game I had had little sleep after finishing at 7 am. I tried my best and ended scoring two tries. Late in the second half I offloaded the ball but was tackled from behind. I extended my arm to brace my fall and crunch! I let out a girlie cry of pain. I was done: I knew I was in serious trouble. It was my first game in eighteen years of rugby where I asked to be taken off. It was so painful I couldn't move my arm.

I went home in pain; the journey took two hours. Exhausted I fell asleep on the District line from Essex to London. I went to the Chelsea and Westminster Hospital for an X-Ray. No break brilliant but I couldn't move my arm. They told me I had suffered a dislocation and they would sedate me to put it back in place. I refused as I was off to Rome the following morning to film the ATP Tennis Masters. I was in a lot of pain, sleeping was horrible. I couldn't even bring my arm across to shower my left armpit; I needed Kirsty to help me shower. My triceps was purple within a day. I should have stayed in hospital, perhaps the treatment would have worked; at least I could have got some sort of attention but I was flying the next day to Rome for work and couldn't afford to be out of it on an anaesthetic.

From then on I didn't play any rugby. I went to the doctor around June time as my shoulder and arm was still stiff. I thought I had just bruised the bone badly as I had done in 2007 at Richmond Rugby club. The doctor wouldn't refer me for an MRI. Apparently my doctor could only refer an MRI for knees and neck problems. I would have to see a physiotherapist; even he didn't know what was wrong with my shoulder so he suggested an MRI was a good idea. I was then referred back to the doctor who now sent me to get one.

It was all a complete waste of time and very frustrating. I told my doctor I would pay for my own MRI but she said the surgeon might not accept it and would want his own MRI. Ridiculous I thought. That September I was supposed to get the scan but the surgeon cancelled and the first available slot was the following February, six months later. I was very frustrated it was still painful to move. It was painful to sleep with as well and sometimes woke me up at night.

Ten months later the MRI confirmed a biceps tendon tear and a partial thickness tear of the subscapularis one of the rotator cuffs.

I had this clunking in my shoulder where the ball was rubbing and grinding against the socket giving a nasty feel and less range of movement. The injury meant there would be no gym or rugby for one year. After diagnosis I received a cortisone injection and a four-month wait for an operation. I was messed about with cancelled NHS appointments, which was very upsetting and frustrating, as I wanted to get on with playing rugby and the rest of my day-to-day life. In fact, I played that summer for a business charity 7s tournament at Rosslyn Park. I avoided contact as much as I could and just hit with my left shoulder. The sun was out and it wasn't a bad day, as I was with a few old school chums, Mark Coombs and Pat Cussens, from Campion School Hornchurch. Kirsty came down to watch as well.

John Rudd had now joined Rosslyn Park. He played at Newcastle Falcons for years with Johnny Wilkinson and now I think he was working in the city as a trader. John went to the same school as me, Campion in Hornchurch and at times we clashed in the playground…me coming off worse of course. But at Rosslyn Park John would take the time to direct me and help me out in terms of what angles to run as a winger. I thought he was a top lad and I appreciated it from an professional player such as himself.

Pre-season came about and in July 2010 I was made redundant. Not a nice experience to say the least but I soon fell on my feet picking up work in the sports television world. I started to miss training due to work with some trips abroad for ATP tennis in the USA and Canada, golf in Austria and Commonwealth Games in Delhi. With my work schedule and the fact I was also in a lot of pain when I pumped my right arm during running, my time at Rosslyn Park RFC was fading. Any time my shoulder was knocked or I had my arm yanked I'd feel it ache severely at training and I'd have to stop momentarily. Before long I was discouraged and stopped playing altogether.

From around December 2010 to summer of 2011 I don't think I played a single game. I did however start training in Battersea Park, next to my house, with London Cornish. Again training proved painful in contact in the English wet weather. I began to get more and more frustrated and being in pain wasn't too pleasant so I stopped training.

In the Summer 2011 the infamous "Net Rugby" was back on Clapham Common, London. A game introduced to me by my former boss with half sized pitches with two poles and netball style hoops on the end. The rules allow you to pass in any direction over or under arm. There is no kicking or shirt pulling and there are no scrums or rucks. There are minimal rules and lots of running. The idea is to get the ball into the opposition net. Simple! Not quite, as it was very brutal but extremely good fitness.

BBC Breakfast came down one week with their presenter and they filmed a short piece about the history of the game and how to play it. There I met a few guys who turned up from a social side called "The Cheeky Ladies". I began to play for "The Cheekies" and played a couple of good games, with my shoulder holding up I tried to make my tackles count. Off the pitch I had a few good socials too. I could run OK but had lost a bit of speed. The main thing I found was I had lost confidence. This was the hardest thing to regain. Taking a blow to the shoulder was painful especially if my arm landed in the wrong way. I felt I had nothing to lose though. I hadn't got high expectations and wasn't too fussed if we lost. In fact I never won with the Cheeky Lady's RFC. One game Kirsty and her parents came down to watch. I loved having spectators supporting. Just having three people fired me up; imagine what having 70,000 odd behind you at Twickenham would do for a player's adrenaline. The home teams club Chairman approached Kirsty's dad. The guy said he would have liked to have invited some of the Cheekies supporters for lunch, thinking Tom was closely related to the team. Now Tom was a bit of a joker. He responded and said "Errr listen, if your food is anything like your crap bar selection I'm glad I didn't come". The bar to be fair was terrible. They ran out of decent ale, didn't stock any whiskey and had no ice. It was a fair comment. Their team was heckling from the sidelines. Tom told them all to be quiet.

I would feel a sharp pain in my shoulder and then a numbing throb. But with two cortisone injections one in April 2011 and again in February 2012. it would settle down quite well; just some backache, I'm guessing from the ligaments damage, or muscle compensation. My job freelancing in the sports world took over and my playing ceased. Luckily though, I would be working filming and editing English Premiership and European cup rugby matches for Sky Sports, the TV network, making montages and analysing passages of play through the shows production with my right hand man Dean Ryan (ex-England) and Scott Quinnel (ex-Wales and British Lions). Some of my mates think it's a dream job and are quite jealous. Great fun but playing was more of a passion than watching although this helped fill the void and the money is great.

Figure 2 Rosslyn Park v Army Regiment 2009

By January 2012 Kirsty and I had been living together for a year. Our relationship was on the rocks and close to being over. I decided I needed to do something. Quite down and depressed I did what Liam always does in times of trouble, I turned back to my sport and fitness. We all know how good we feel after a run or gym session. I tried to get myself back in shape but, as painful as it is to say, I hit the booze and cigarettes pretty hard as I was depressed about my break up with Kirsty. I would go out and get drunk three to four times a week and smoke a pack a day. My fitness was lacking severely. The gym stopped and the long 10km late night runs ceased. After briefly being back together again we ended things pretty badly. At the same time a good friend of mine from my University days of 1999 died suddenly. Matt was an American exchange student. We made friends after I had finished a summer camp program in New York in 1999 and returned to the UK for studying. I had worked the whole season 2011-12 as hard as I could. I had saved a lot of money and been smart with my freelance business. I decided it was time to make one last effort to play rugby. Life seemed too short. Was Matt the whole reason for going away to play rugby? Perhaps not but it certainly inspired me to take life by the horns. It certainly contributed to it so I thank him for leaving me with some hope of my future. Was I fed up with work and needed a break? Yes probably. Was I trying to fill the void of something missing? I don't know but I wanted the love from my teammates. I missed Doc, Anthony and Daniel my rugby mates in Florida. We had been through a lot in 2008. I always loved that camaraderie from a team; the bonding that took place...I wanted something more. I wanted to get out of my comfort zone, fly thousands of miles and train and train my heart out. Make sacrifices that I knew I would one day be proud of. I knew I could do it and that I wanted it. I knew once there I would be around a special group of people that I loved.

I would call Brian the coach in Florida and come over in June 2012. I wasn't really thinking about Nationals at the time. I wanted to play rugby and for the trip to coincide with my birthday. I cancelled working on the European football championship from the studios in London as well. I cancelled working eighteen days on the Olympics in London worth around £6500, although I did have another confirmed booking filming European golf in Austria at the start of the games.

I emailed Lauren Scharmek whose dad works for Delta Air. Lauren was dating Ben Catania a fine athlete. Ben's style was almost like Ben Foden's of England. He would make great lines and had a powerful sidestep. Ben was a strong tackler too, with great acceleration and top speed. I admired him as a rugby player. After hooking me up with a non-revenue ticket for £450,

I would make some final training preparations although I thought it would be easier mentally for me to just show up. I didn't want any pressure or mind set to kick in for the first part. I wanted to be relaxed. I flew out June 14th and was unable to make the Thursday night training with the Daytona Beach rugby guys as the flight arrived so late. The next day on Friday we travelled down to West Palm Beach around three hours drive south of Daytona. We trained in the evening. It hurt me. It was the belting heat and humidity that I was not use to.

Saturday arrived, the day of the tournament. I hadn't played for Daytona in four years. We had two sides. I started in the second side quite happily. I met a new bunch of guys and was fairly impressed. We had some size this time. Leon was South African. He looked like he could play scrum half, prop, centre. Moose with his military background seemed like he could run all day. Other players like Matt McGuiness and "Alaska" Jeff Herron looked useful. I met a chap called Cagney. He resembled Keith Wood the Irish hooker. He was mobile and got around the park well and nice guy too good sense of humour, which can be rare for an America. Dan Palmer my old "Pedigree chum" from 2008 and Mark Eichner were looking sharp. I was extremely excited to play along side them. I never knew Mark in 2008 at Nationals and to be honest I wasn't a great fan at the time. He was like a moody student moping around. I've told him this and the summer of 2012 he turned out to be my wingman personal chauffeur and I hope great lasting friend. A Kenyan lad started studying at the University of Embry Riddle. Kenny was fast. He had great endurance and most importantly he knew the game well.

Young Joe a student and track runner at Embry Riddle the Aeronautical University in Daytona was putting away a few tries on the wing. I set up a fair few tries then in my second game I came on as a sub against UCF (University Central Florida). A quick dummy scissors pop and I was away slicing the defence in

30

half running thirty meters to score. Oh the joy of exorcising those demons was finally done. I had not scored a club try since 2010 before I hurt my shoulder. I was back and I knew it. I nearly cried. I had the world's biggest smile and I let Doc know just how happy I was. I played a few games at scrum half for Doc who seemed to be either hurt or resting. I did split my ear, well between my ear and temple. I was a bit worried as they said it looked deep but the physio glued it up and added some steri-strips. They bandaged me up and also Doc gave me his head guard. I had no excuses and was going to go for it.

Ben unfortunately got hurt. It was a real blow for him and also the team. I had seen his Facebook updates over the last three years about rugby and training and because of his girlfriend I had got a cheap flight over last minute. Mark later got injured and his knee got twisted badly. Both Ben's and Mark's injuries seemed quite bad. Mark would be nurturing his injury all summer and would miss the end of that day's rugby. It was the same for Ben.

I ended up scoring 3 tries that day and I left the field quite chuffed. I had come over with nothing, played and made my way to the First team. I had ended up captaining the final and winning the tournament for the team. This earned me a MVP (Most Valuable Player) Daytona Beach beer cup. I was very proud. Not just that I could still play rugby, but I had done well, scored a few points, played an important role, captained the side and also filled one of my favourite players position. Taking the place of James Brown was a very proud moment for me indeed and I think by the smile on my face he knew that too.

Two weeks later we would play at the Todd Miller tournament in Orlando. I took a week off training. Perhaps slightly too much partying but the next week it was back to the hard running and gym. Training was tough even at 6-8 pm in the evening. The humidity was still there as was the heat. My training shirt would be dripping wet and I would have to wring it out. It made the ball slippery and defending would be tough constantly moving right to left, then back to the right. Brian would make us play 7 against 10 and sometimes it proved frustrating. Doc or I would get frustrated, do things in training that perhaps we wouldn't do in a game. I struggled to pass off my right hand to my right probably because I was out of sync with ball and body or maybe because of my shoulder injury. This made it more frustrating for me as I looked bad.

At the Todd Miller tournament on June 30th 2012 I had made the twelve-man squad and would play at fly half and scrum half. I didn't really know how hard scrum half was. I knew I would have to get under the skin of my opposite number. I was a pain in the arse to him. I would not allow the scrum half to put the ball in I would push him or tread on his foot to put him off. Coach Brian hated this but it was my way of not taking a backward step in what I thought was a position I wasn't necessarily suited to. I made it difficult for the scrum half to pass out clean ball or I would at least try to smash him and take him out the game. On a day where Dan, Ben and Mark didn't feature I ended up scoring 7 tries. Kenny looked like a good player, running hard and scoring a few too. He was fast and strong even for a skinny guy. Anthony Muniz, my old friend from Nationals who I played with in 2008, was playing for Orlando in the tournament. He would call me Casper legs as I was still looking like a pale Englishman. "Casper the little friendly ghost" he would say which made me laugh. I've been called a lot worse I thought. It was a shame not to play along side him or even against him. We eventually, after waiting a while, made the final. I didn't play that well against Cabana RFC and was brought off. It was maybe a fair call as I was probably tired by half time. Joe our little winger tried many times to get round the Cabana RFC winger but was stopped dead in his tracks. But the little guy didn't give up and it was on the other wing that he raced round his man to score in the dying seconds to win us the tournament, as I watched from the sideline. Another piece of silverware banked.

So I was supposed to leave for the UK on July 2nd and come back for the South Final Championship July 22nd. It would be the best teams from Florida, Georgia, Louisiana and the Carolinas. If we won this we would qualify for Nationals. I decided to stay in Daytona and Brian agreed for me to stay with him and his family. It was free and after a small upset at Doc's place with his live in girlfriend I found myself happy settled and helping Brian plan the back room stuff for hosting the South Finals. Brian was a busy man always emailing, phone calling or just planning. He was a high school careers mentor and as school was done for the summer this allowed him to use his time to plan the rugby. He ran the club single-handedly and for some time I admired that. I then saw how difficult he made it. I wanted to help but he would not explain anything to me. None of the other players took into consideration what he was doing. To host a rugby tournament you need a field, that goes without saying, players team (that helps), match balls, referees, insurance at where you play, first aid, tents for the teams, printed tickets for the public, hundreds of bottles of water, snacks, a roped area, lavatories. We wanted to make this an annual event so teams would come back each year. The founder, Gerry Keating, who is a lawyer, knew a law firm who did a lot of PR work and had a printing company make us leaflets and tickets for free. I bought a local newspaper advert. We put two signs up on the main Granada Bridge with the city council's permission. We had a free radio commercial with a sexy voiced lady announce the tournament and event. We organised a post match 7 bar pub-crawl. For this we would need to convince the bars to sponsor us without making them donate money. We just needed agreement for drinks specials if we promised them punters. Mark and I helped promote this by going in and speaking to the bar managers often getting turned right down.

Others were sketchy, wanting to check with the owners. Eventually we had 7 sign up with various drink specials for players and fans with tickets.

I trained hard in the gym and did several track sessions, running repeat 400 meters laps making good times in the baking Florida sunshine. I wanted to be conditioned although I should have done this pre season. The thing was, I didn't have a pre season. It was pretty much lastminute.com for me when I made the choice to go and play in Florida. The last session I started getting backaches. It was only one week before the South Finals. I had no idea why; I didn't think I was over training. It was more like muscle spasms and I got it when I moved a certain way, moved or ran. I had to stop at rugby practice and felt I couldn't run. This had never happened before and I felt defeated taking myself out of a session. Mark was ushering me to get into position, as my defence was shoddy. I just couldn't move around the training field as I wanted. Had I over-trained or was it the beds I was sleeping in. I mean I had slept in a few beds from the places I was being put up in. I took myself out fearing something was definitely wrong. I iced it and used an icy hot patch for a few days. I thought that maybe I wouldn't play; I had no idea how many days it would feel like that. The problem faded around the fourth day but it had made me anxious and it had troubled me.

However, I was getting slightly restless in general. It was now the second week of July. Maybe I was homesick. Maybe I missed Kirsty and needed her comfort. Maybe I was taking it for granted how lucky I was just being there? There were a lot of maybes and a lot of mixed emotions about everything that crossed my mind. However I did love the fact that I was once again in my life eating, breathing and sleeping rugby. It was brilliant just like my new family. It was just hard to get hold of people though. No one would call or text me as they said it was too expensive. I had no way of getting around without asking people and I started to feel my independence was far out the window to what I was used to for so many years in London.

The night before the South Finals I desperately had no idea where I was staying. I didn't get to bed until 2 am that wasn't ideal with a 7.30 am rise. I was still sore from training hard that week and extremely physically tired. I was mad at Brian, as my head was a mess because I didn't know where I was staying. In the end his kind wife Becky helped me to the hotel. Our friendship, myself as the player and Brian as "The Boss", as he liked to be called, in my opinion started to wear a little thin.

The day of the South Finals I kept saying, "Wake up, get yourself together". I didn't get much game time although I did OK in some games. To be honest it was so hot that day and I was shattered I don't really remember much. Mark's knee was bad but he played on as Dan was rested.

I remember mentoring Joe. He was upset his brother was playing 3rd side and that Brian had not picked him. Joe and Anthony were brothers one year apart. They were from New York and looked out for each other well. I explained to Joe that this was a special day for him as an individual and not to worry about Brian or his brother. I told him that this was his day to shine and to succeed and to not let anything else get in his way. Stay focussed on the job I told him. He was very grateful and went on to deliver well. I played in the final against Charlotte. I came on with three and half minutes to go. They had a scrum on the left side. Joe was defending the right side of the pitch at wing and I was what you may call a blind side wing with about 20 meters to the touchline. I knew the guy opposite me was talented. I tried calling Mark to switch as I doubted myself and panicked. The ball went blind to him off their put in. I showed him the touchline and he took it. He ran at me and made a split second jerk, then he took off round the corner. My hips were too square and I could not shift to catch him. He went on to score. Charlotte had now levelled the score. My heart sank. What had I done? Did I just blow my team's chance of going to the National finals? Did I just shatter a dozen people's dreams? It was honestly my worst fear and moment in the 21 years of playing rugby. They then had the kick off and luckily for us it went out on the full. This gave us a free kick on the half way line under 7s rugby rules. Moose took off and tossed the ball wide to my side. I went to catch it but pulled out. I had a feeling by the way the ball was coming towards me at the speed it was that it wasn't meant for me - it was Joe's ball. He took the outside. I followed close behind Joe pumping my arms. Somewhere I had got my legs back and was in support. He didn't need me and ran it in from the touchline to under the posts. I hugged him dearly for what he had done. Thank you Joe for scoring. Thank you for just erasing my horrible error. I asked the ref for the time left on the clock. We were up 5 points but she said after the conversion that was it, that the game would be over. Doc allowed me to take the conversion. The ball sailed over and I was happy to go back home to the UK knowing I had scored some points. Scoring maybe not the most important points ever but at least the last two points before Nationals. Joe became an instant Hero. I can't explain how relieved I was for it to be over. Joe had scored another last minute try to win us 2012 South Finals Rugby Championship. California here we come.

But I was still anxious. I needed to be alone. I was sad. There were so many mixed feelings. I had accomplished being part of a winning South Finals team and was set to go to Nationals again, yet I felt I hadn't earned it. Was I just lucky to be on that Daytona 1st team? Was I just an extra to make up the team somehow by default? Had I really helped them get to Nationals? I never used to ask these questions, I just enjoyed playing. I just enjoyed the buzz and never took it so seriously. I broke down in the bathroom while everyone celebrated. I wasn't there for the trophy lift or the captain's speech, which I now regret. But I just felt I hadn't been given the chance to do what I desperately thought I could do. Maybe I just desperately wanted to do it and couldn't...and wasn't picked because Brian thought I wasn't capable.

Whatever the answers to the above, Brian and Daytona Beach rugby were going to San Francisco for 2012 National Rugby 7s Finals for the first time since 2008. For a small city with many social issues drug related, poverty and low-level income that the tourists don't see, this was a big thing for a small team with low funding but a massive milestone for such a small group of people with big hearts.

I called my agency in the UK who find me work and cancelled all the dates for working on the reality TV show Big Brother for the month of August.

The day after the South Finals I flew back to London. I had to connect in New York. If I missed my NY flight I was worried I wouldn't make it back to the UK. I was living on the edge, juggling because the following day I was flying out to Austria. The client had booked and paid for a group booking. I would be in great trouble if I didn't make that flight to arrive in Austria to start work.

I had one day back in London then I was in Austria for six days of work on the European golf tour, broadcasting to the world from 40 miles outside Vienna.

I returned from Austria and then had three days in London where my best friend Ben Mosquera came over from Russia with his wife. I knew Ben from 1999 and it was Ben that I moved to Florida with originally in 2001. I had missed the wedding the previous year so it was great to have them stay and meet his wife. I booked my flight to Nationals costing me £1500 flying Virgin Atlantic. I was lucky to have Upper Class on the outbound to San Fran. It would also be my rugby friend Andy Dilsaver's wedding the following week. I made sure the flight flew back to London from LAX, I mean I was in California anyway. I missed his last wedding what would one more week cost me in life? So I decided that after the rugby was finished I'd make my way to Los Angeles for the wedding. It would be a good thing to do and I was excited for him. But Nationals was my main concern. I knew from the South Finals I would be covering scrum half, fly half and centre for injuries. I thought I would be given game time. I had sacrificed a huge sum of money and spent a lot too. For both Trans-Atlantic trips I funded myself I would go on to fly 16,000 miles in total.

I arrived in style. The only flights direct to San Francisco from London were with Virgin Atlantic. I could have gone a day later, had to connect in New York and it would have arrived late evening. But, I wanted to be fresh come the Thursday, to train and be with the team.

Unfortunately no one came to pick me up. I was told in three different emails which hotel we were at and when I arrived I then received a Facebook message from coach Brian that Ryan one of the players would pick me up. I knew Ryan but I had no contact for him not even Facebook. I waited half an hour then made my way via public transport south of San Francisco to Belmont a suburb. I waited for about 45 minutes in the warm San Fran afternoon sun on my back for a train. I finally boarded but I realised I had perhaps gone too far and to my suspicion I worked out that I was on the fast train and I had already passed my destination. Quite annoyed I arrived in San Jose and asked about a cab. I wasn't going to pay the $70; it was only $25 originally from the airport. The rest of the guys arriving didn't have reception, which suggested they were still flying.

Three hours later after landing, Brian with his hired mini van Mark, Joe and Dwayne came to get me. Not exactly very impressed with the organisation and communication, we then drove back to the airport to pick someone up. I was quite annoyed to say the least. We went for food and I fell asleep around 7 pm as my body was thinking it to be 3 am UK time.

We checked in to some shit hole motel that smelt of marijuana. I was bunking with Mark. I went to bed and I passed out immediately. Dan arrived at 2 am and I just managed to say hi. It was good to see him again but then I fell asleep.

The next day some more of the guys arrived. We went to Muir National Park. I felt a bit down. I felt tired and flat and it wasn't like being at a National rugby final. I picked up a bit during the day. We trained in the evening and I wasn't really featured in any attacking line up or what would seem any line up at all which started to concern me about being selected.

We all moved to another hotel. I was concerned about sleeping arrangements. I was supposed to be staying with Mark and Dan but felt like, as their girlfriends were there, that I was a spare wheel. I spoke to Mark and his answer was that we would figure it out. In hindsight I should have told them my concerns but I went to Brian and asked him to make sure I was able to sleep in a room comfortably. I was shattered the night before the South Finals and I slept on the floor at Nationals in 2008 sacrificing for Doc and Dan to get some rest as our star players. This time it backfired and Dan was upset. We argued but instead of shouting and responding I tried to keep calm. Words were used and Dan decided to move out with his girlfriend to another room. I was quite upset but felt Dan was over reacting. I just felt it was unfair people that weren't playing rugby were taking beds when donations had been made for the team. And I felt like I was owed something for all the travelling, costs and work I'd given up. It just caused me trouble.

On the Friday we went to register at Golden Gate rugby club. There I met Al Caravelli former USA Eagles 7s coach. We looked at the pitch for a bit but that was about it as far as I remember. Perry arrived and then Mark moved out of the room. I didn't socialise that day; they all went downtown to do touristy stuff. I was too sad and down because Dan and Mark had both left the room. I felt like everyone was against me, that I had caused upset. I felt like an outcast but maybe it was my own doing. It was a very tough day for sure. I wanted to tell Brian I had made a mistake coming, good luck and that I was leaving the group. I really don't know why I was so down. I knew someone else from Florida could have had my position and I would have squandered the right to be there. I kept saying don't do anything stupid you are upset right now but it will be fine tomorrow. I remember hearing Dean Ryan at work on a Sky Sports job once. What he said had stayed in my head and I remembered it momentarily at the hotel in San Francisco. He was speaking about an incident between player and coach and said it's not what happens in a situation but how one conducts himself that will determine how well you move forward. That was on my mind all the time. That night we had all got together. We ate dinner, drank lots of fluids and had a team talk. I had prepared a few words but sat in the corner and kept quiet. With all my playing years I felt I should have some inspirational words to say about how there wouldn't be another chance at this title, about how many people were rooting for us and about how far we had come. The night before I captained my University team I summoned everyone to a short team meeting. I went through keywords like communication, discipline, defence, and ruthlessness. It obviously worked as we went on to win. This was a different scenario and I felt it wasn't my place to speak as a leader...after all I was just a sub. Then we all went to bed around 11 pm for an early night.

Saturday dawned. It was now day one of Nationals. Was I nervous? Yes! We all had breakfast. We jumped in the mini bus and I was going over in my head mentally scenarios where I may have to come on for an injury at one of the positions. Our first game was against Youngbludz who had finished 4th the previous year. We lost and I didn't feature. Game 2 was against Old Puget Sound from Washington State. None other than Waisale Serevi himself was coaching the team. Ben Golllings, the highest scoring 7s rugby player ever was also associated with their team. I had a chat with Ben - he seemed very conversational. We spoke about his team and his own rugby and what he was doing now in his life. Old Puget Sound RFC were great rugby players as well as athletes. We let 2 soft tries in but scored one. Game on though I thought! Then they put 2 more on us. In the dying seconds, when I knew the game was over, I asked Brian please to put me on if just for some game time. He responded by telling me "Fuck off and to get the fuck out of here." Mortified I wanted to throw in the towel. Silencing me is a rare thing. Not many people do that. It doesn't happen that often. Maybe I thought I had actually been out of line. I thought best to bite my tongue. I was angry and embarrassed by what had happened on the sideline but I had to go with it. I would not have done this at any other level. I remember playing for Manchester RFC a semi pro side in the UK. The game was against Sale academy, the academy side of the Premiership club. I was on the bench and Baldwin the head coach wouldn't play me. He kept even subbing the subs instead of me. I was deeply upset but I accepted it. He was kind enough to pull me aside and explain why, almost as an apology. I liked that and I appreciated it. This didn't happen to me this time so I just acted like nothing had happened kept quiet and tried to focus on the next game in case I was picked. The third game we played against Maryland Exiles. I played at Scrum half and did quite a good job. I played the first half and a minute of the 2nd half. I really battled against my opposite number and gave him a hard time. One tackle resulted I believe with a boot to his face, at least although I had no idea at the time until I saw the pictures posted online. I took a quick tap penalty five meters out. It was two on two. I sucked them both in and then zipped out a pass to Dwayne. He went over to score. Game won. After Day one we had played 3, lost 2 and won 1. I was pretty happy with my performance as another pass set up Rod to score too although he had a bit more work to do to score than Dwayne. One player had yelled at me after the try was awarded because he wanted the ball to go open with a four on four option. I backed our chances with the blind side drawing the defender and making a two on two become a two on one.

We were now playing for positions 9-16. Ok it wasn't as good as 2008 but that game against Youngbluz was crucial and we had to move on. I believed all summer we were slow to start and with that early 10.40 am kick off maybe that's why. But we were in the bowl knock out stage and we could at least finish still with some silverware. We went back home to the hotel and dinner was provided. I slept in the room with Perry Baker we packed all our stuff and prepared for the second day. I slept pretty well and woke up feeling good about the day.

Our first game of Day 2 was against Kansas City Blues. I came on with 2-3 minutes to go. Dan Palmer scored an amazing try but hurt his ankle in the process and needed serious treatment. It finished off his weekend ending with him on crutches. It was all level as they scored in the dying seconds. I had a chance with our scrum that we won, to kick the ball dead but I had not asked the ref if there was time on the clock and we allowed them to score, to level the game at full time. It went into sudden death. We had used all our subs. Somehow Joe got the ball and raced to score which meant we were in the semi finals against Charlotte a few hours later. Yet again little Joe saved us and brought home the bacon. We had played Charlotte twice at the South Finals. They had beaten us in the first game but we had won in the dying seconds by you name it, yes that man Joe DiGregorio who always seemed to score when we most needed him to. Charlotte had looked good all day in my opinion, beating some tough teams. We managed to hold out well and won the match putting us in the final against OMBAC (Old Missions Beach Athletic Club) based in San Diego.

I didn't play in the final but it looked pretty tough. Ryan Shore showing some brilliance in the air from the kick offs. Doc's and

Mark's long-term injuries were holding up well, although Doc was complaining about a groin strain, he was soldiering on. Everyone had come too far to turn back now. If I remember Perry Baker ran many down the touchline and would cut breaking the tackles to run and score under the posts. This got the attention of many spectators and even the National coach dragged Perry aside for an invitation to the USA National Eagles tryouts. We had won the National bowl and finished 9th place out of the top 16 teams. I had many mixed emotions about it. I was happy for the team, the players, the coach and the support. I just didn't feel I contributed much to the winning. It was later I spoke to Isaac Coudurier a young player from Nationals in 2008 who, like me, did not get much game time. He told me that I would have contributed a great deal getting the team to Nationals from previous tournaments. This helped me see things in a slightly different perspective.

But at the time, I didn't really feel the win. I didn't even want to hold the bowl as pretty as it was. I felt like I hadn't earned the right to hold it. I felt like I didn't want to take the credit for other people's accomplishments. I felt I never had the opportunity to give something on the field. Every game, every warm up I gave the same approach. All the mental build-ups preparing myself, mentoring myself, calming myself down, telling myself, as Sean Fitzpatrick tells people, to be the best I could be for the team. It was hard on the sidelines acting as chief water boy only to look on. Mark always seemed to do well, as did Ryan. Every time I heard Brian say "Leon warm up" I thought he would say "Liam" and my heart would sink when I realised it wasn't me he wanted to go on. To not play and have the disappointment each game was almost heart breaking.

I felt that after my girl friend and I broke up I would fill the gap with the rugby tour. I had started to doubt it and doubt myself. I had given up a lot of things and expected things back, which was against what my Mum and Dad had taught me. The hour before the final I went for a walk. I had to get away and think about things. I was pretty fragile and almost gave up. I listened to a voice message from Kirsty that I had saved. It was almost two minutes long. She told me that she was so pleased for me that I was achieving so well with all the rugby tournaments I had played in that summer. She went on to say that earlier in the year, she remembered me speaking about perhaps going but wasn't too sure because of my fitness. She said that she was so pleased for me for doing what I believed to be possible. She told me that I never gave up and that was one thing she loved about me. Apparently this had also inspired her to do well. She said she would go for runs after work tired but not give up because something from me had rubbed off on to her. It was a nice inspiring message for me to pick myself up. But the one person in life that knew me inside out wasn't part of my life anymore and that hurt.

I wanted to play so badly and the torment of not being given the chance to do so was killing me. Being a sub was something I wasn't used to. I was not comfortable being on the bench...not playing was something that hurt me and dented my pride. If I had been a sub all the time I would have been used to it. Once at University in 2003 Ben Barlow the captain said. "OK I am playing you the first half, make something happen as I'm bringing you off at half time for Richard Todd" This inspired me to do well and do exactly what he told me. I found myself at fly-half 5 meters out and went over to score.

As the tournament was over we had a few beers. Except I didn't because I just hadn't felt I had earned them. I couldn't bring myself to celebrate, as I had not contributed. To make matters worse I hadn't stood up for the American National Anthem of the final. Two players objected and classed me as disrespectful. It was a fucking joke in my eyes. I had never been part of such a team in my life. We were supposed to be all mates. I thought I had made those sacrifices like everyone else. But even off the field I seemed to cause problems. I felt like I had felt at school when I wasn't included in the team. 16 years later and probably my final era of playing I felt like an outcast by a couple of individuals.

We took some pictures over looking San Francisco, packed up and drove home. I felt uncomfortable and was quiet. I had no jokes or smiles for anyone. It was a very weird feeling that I've never had coming off the rugby field. I was pleased for Doc and some others. I said goodbye to Mark. Mark had been my wingman, my drinking buddy and my chauffeur all summer. I promised him a place to stay if he wanted to come to London. I said goodbye to Dan for the last time. We both said sorry, put away our differences and hugged. It was a nice moment for me to see a good man start the rest of his life with his new career as a fire fighter ahead of him in Colorado. I liked Dan he was fun, passionate about rugby and a good honest man. We drove and checked into a new hotel downtown. Moose and Alaska were in one bed, Rod and myself in another. Doc did however say how much he appreciated my efforts of flying all that way over, he said he never had a chance to say thanks all summer but truly meant it. He had been busy with his medical practice and we had not really hung out like the old days but I understood. He was a good man and I appreciated his thank you. I relaxed a little and warmed to the guys I thought had been a bit distant to me. We partied hard in a few bars in San Francisco. Included in the group were Ryan and his wife, Doc, Stephanie, Rod, myself, Moose and Alaska. Rod and I arrived back at the hotel around 5 am only for him to leave at 6 am for his flight back to Atlanta.

The next day, I took in some of the fresh city air and made my way to the airport to fly to Los Angeles to see my friend, Andy, get married. The rugby was now over. I thought, well I've come this fair, given up so much work I may as well take another week off to see Andy get married. I missed his last one there might not be another one. Andy had been my mate for 11 years.

He had kept in touch and had invited Kirsty and me the year before. I had visited him a number of times in the USA and he had travelled to London too to stay and party with me. It was rugby that had brought us together as mates so I was excited to witness a special moment of his life. Truth be told, I couldn't wait to leave San Fran. Brian was with Doc in another hotel and everyone else had left early that morning or the night before. I felt lonely and a bit isolated. I really couldn't wait to leave. There was nothing left for me in San Francisco. I hadn't enjoyed being there from the start. I decided to write a poem about how I felt. I'm not quite sure the reason but I did. I hadn't written one since my school days but this is what it said. I think it's rather self-explanatory.

I was your cushion when you would fall
I was the one patiently waiting for my time of call
I was plan C when A and B were done
Just give me the word a chance to go and run
I was there to give you hope to quench your thirst and shout
cheers
From the sidelines anxious and desperate were my worst fears
Each warm up, the same intense mental state I would gain
Each second of the clock I'm listening out for my name
But the job was done fine no more chances to play
Bowl champions as I write a chapter when leaving the San Fran
Bay.

So now I'm back in the UK. Was I glad I went? Yes! Did I achieve what I wanted to achieve? Maybe? Maybe not! Maybe I achieved something else that I haven't yet realised. What I do know is that I never thought I would play again at the USA National Finals. I did not even think I was going to play at a high level anywhere due to my work lifestyle and my injured shoulder. Doc even admitted that maybe it was a fluke in 2008 to get there let alone come 5th position to win the Plate. Of course it showed I was able to change my lifestyle, to do something good for the team, for myself and for my own life. People helped me on the way but it showed how I was able to make something happen. I took a gamble with the two trips and juggled work. It was stressful yes. Especially the flights, the different time zones and the moving around so much. But it was another example of getting out of my comfort zone to try and achieve something. It's about having a vision and going for it. And that's exactly what I did.

Looking forward now though, I think my time is done flying to the USA for serious rugby tours at National level. We certainly had a deep team where players could interchange positions within the forwards and backs, something that we didn't have in 2008. The opposition has definitely become better as the game advances and progresses in the USA. The career thing was a one off taking a break like that. I'd still love to play especially at a semi pro club here in London but due to working I simply can't afford to take Saturdays off. It has given me encouragement in life for sure. The old saying to enjoy the rainbow one must accept the rain is very true. A friend once told me we always have hope and this is also very true. Hope is stronger than fear. A little hope is not enough but a lot of hope can be more powerful than one can imagine.

Figure 3 Daytona win 9th place at the USA National 7s finals 2012

Figure 4 Playing scrum half attacking my opposite number at the USA National 7s final 2012

Chapter 4

So where did it all start? It's hard to remember. Where did I get this determination from, this drive to do better and to win at all costs?

Mum was a musician and opera singer she never played sports with me. Dad claimed to have played 1st team rugby at school but I wasn't convinced. Maybe my Mum's competitive drive to win auditions and to practice and succeed was passed down to me. My Grandmother had left Italy with nothing and built up a small financial empire; did I get this drive from her? My Dad was logical. Perhaps his ability to analyse situations helped me make decisions under pressure on the pitch? I do remember that if I was left out of the games at school, whether being cricket, rugby or football I would be gutted. I always believed that I had some talent even if others didn't. I wasn't the best but I could be pretty handy. I do remember a few times being a hero in the class cricket team. Taking wickets as a somewhat spin bowler or making a fine catch at silly mid off but I don't recall ever scoring a winning try at school.

It would have been around 1984. I would be joining St. John Fisher Primary School the following year. It was at my sister's sports day. There was a make shift race organised for the smaller younger children. I would take part and apparently I barged all the other kids out the way to get to the finish line first. It was just an instinct I guess. I never considered myself that fast of a runner. When playing rugby I was always scared of getting hurt so it was down to me to get away from the guy as quick as possible. I certainly didn't like getting tackled as a young boy…for a skinny lad like me it hurt. I remember I was always such a big football fan supporting the Tottenham Hotspurs because one of my friends from school when I was 7 told me about them. We also had a sports store owned by Glen Hoddle in my hometown. We would play in the playground at school everyday, twice a day and by the time Italia 90 World Cup came around we were playing Italy v Ireland, replicating the famous game that the Irish won. I could have played for both teams given my background from my mother and father. I would play every Saturday with the cub's team in Loughton until I was 10-11.

The summer of 1990 I would practise kick ups or "keepy upies" in the garden with my coca-cola soccer ball, not doing too well.

In 1991 I started secondary school. I took a bunch of exams for private schools. It was a scary experience plus I was being told I would have to take a long journey via trains, underground and bus to get there.

My father took me to Campion School in Hornchurch, Essex. My first reaction when I saw the amount of playing fields was "Corrrrrrrrre" I was amazed. Maybe 6 football pitches 8 rugby pitches I couldn't be certain. Dad had briefly taken me to see The Campion Old Boys' rugby team vs. London Irish Amateurs. It was raining. I was bored and cold on the sideline heckling and being a bit of a yob no doubt. I remember kicking my soccer ball around on the side not that interested except when 2 players smashed into each other.

I remember England played Scotland in the spring of 1991 and Dad went with a friend or with work. He showed me one player, Damian Cronin from Bath and Scotland used to attend Campion School and I was impressed a bit as I had the programme Dad had given me as a souvenir.

That September 1991, I started school at Campion and also had my first taste of playing rugby. We all had our new maroon coloured playing kits. We would run around in painted grids passing the ball in all directions. We learnt the basics of tackling and the game itself. One thing stood out. I was told it was a contact sport. I was allowed to get hurt but I was not allowed to moan about it. Other phrases like "Give a good pass, a sympathetic pass," was a phrase always used by our teacher.

Hearing this from my teacher has always been embedded in my head. I remember looking through the yearbook calendar of all the teams we would play against. Some of the teams would be local and some miles away. There would be two buses one leaving from Upminster Bridge and one from Brentwood. My Dad would have to drive me to school and then pick me up. Other times we would drive straight there, if they were halfway across London or the other side.

That autumn of 1991 England would host the World Cup. I started getting into rugby a bit at school. Dad had some tickets for the World Cup matches. One was USA v Italy up in Otley, Yorkshire. By this time my cousin from New Zealand was here. We drove up from Essex around 4 hours and I remember the small ground/stadium was at the bottom of a hill almost at the bottom of a small looking valley. I took my Italian flag to wave although I didn't know any of the players I was right down on the touchline. I remember everyone was rooting for the Americans shouting, "Come on USA" in a funny northern accent. I thought I was going to be beaten up by this weird sounding northerner in his mid 20's telling me to get rid of that flag.

The next game Dad and I went to Leicester. It was Italy vs. New Zealand. This was a bigger stadium and again I took my flag that had been given to me by a guy from the Catholic Church I served at. There were many more people there and more Italian supporters also with big flags like mine. Dad told me to get on TV in front of one of the cameras.

My cousin bought me an Adidas William Web Ellis ball. I had no idea who William Web Ellis was and as we know he was the first guy to pick up a football at Rugby School and start running with it. I would take the ball to the park and kick it about mindlessly. I wasn't too sure why it would bobble around so much unlike a conventional football. It was easy to kick it on its flatter side but I didn't like kicking it on the tip. I was only 11 years old and it hurt my foot too much. At school I started learning how to use a computer. I would play about with it as it had graphics software. I tried to replicate the ticket I had as a souvenir with the IRB (International Rugby Board) logo along with the ball and Gilbert logo that was on my ticket.

We also once had a school trip for those who liked rugby and we all got a bus to Twickenham from the school. It seemed to take forever. It was for the game of New Zealand vs. England. Again it was just a chance for me to misbehave and have fun. I was heckling at Kiwi fans with their flags. I watched as my Head of Year's patience was wearing thin but as my Dad was present there wasn't much he could say or much he could do to discipline me. Liam 1…Mr Adams 0.

Back to playing rather than spectating, around this time I remember that I was a small lad. However I was quick and the thought of someone chasing me scared the hell out of me. It fuelled me to get away from them, away from the danger or getting hurt.

Dad would tell me to be scrum half or hooker, that way I would get to touch the ball more often. He would tell me to smash the other scrum half but he and I had not realised it was against the rules for our age group. You had to allow the scrum half to pass freely. We would play tackle rugby in sports lesson without boots. I thought this was a bit soft. One lesson was so cold John O' Donnell and I were both close to tears. Our fingers felt frozen and I remember being belted with hailstones during class. Not nice but I'm sure it was good character building for a young lad. I learnt my fingers would be warm under my armpits or down my pants between my family jewels. One lesson I made a superb tackle jumping from behind and grasping his ankles by holding on for dear life. I was told that it was an international tackle. All the other better, players seemed jealous but I was very proud and extremely honoured by the teacher when he told me that.

I remember our PE class well. One week we would have swimming and the other week we would have rugby skills in the playground, on the concrete surface. On one occasion, two lads forgot their PE kit. No one knew about the "scank tank" at this stage of our school life. The "scank tank" was a rubbish bin full of old sports clothes people had left behind full of mud, ripped and generally not nice to wear. On this occasion the two lads, David Terris and John Cannon, were made to play rugby in their Speedos. It was rather hilarious to the rest of us and highly amusing. In this day and age though it is probably very illegal now for a teacher to discipline a child in that fashion. I'm not sure you can discipline a child in that way for forgetting the correct attire for a PE class.

I started making the year 1st team although I did not really get on with guys from the other classes in the year. I was fairly small. Quite skinny and didn't like getting hurt. I was never great at tackling.

We were all told time and time again never to kick a rugby ball. I guess they wanted our passing skills to be so slick. I was even told by one teacher that it was the 11th Commandment. "Thou shall not kick a rugby ball". I think I probably believed him. Yet some players could kick it for what seemed miles. Before rugby lesson we would kick the ball around if you were brave enough to leave the warmth of the changing rooms. Sometimes the grounds seemed hard as rock the other times it would be a sea of mud. But whatever happened we would be playing rugby regardless of the weather. It was a school tradition and they were very proud of their rugby.

We would start the lesson with a warm up run to let off some steam. I would always push through but come in the top 15-25 of the year, sometimes in the top 10 trying not to cut corners and cheat myself. We would warm up with passing drills moving around and getting our selves ready to play. We then might play a game of some sort or do some tackling practice.

By the time I was in 4th-5th year, I had made the top team in the year. Rhys Pit was the captain and he wasn't a fan of me. He told me to just get out the way and to stay at fullback. I thought this was pretty harsh but it turned out to be a blessing in disguise. This would be the start of my fullback days. I remember tackling and making a try saving tackle. I even managed to tackle one guy even though I had suffered a broken knuckle from a fight non-rugby related I had had with another student the week before. I felt pretty tough at the time.

In my last year we were allowed the chance to play football or rugby. I choose football, although the teachers advised me that I had talent and I should stick to rugby. I disagreed and was proud of wearing my Italy football shirt thinking I would play in the football World Cup one day. We didn't play against other schools. It was fun to play football but I don't really know how much I got out of it. Perhaps my teachers were right with their advice.

I left that school in 1996 and joined a new school but didn't play for my sixth form, as there wasn't a rugby team. I wondered if I had made the right decision.

Chapter 5

Around 1994-5 I did, however, start playing for a local club. John O' Donnell, a classmate who I would get the train with half way home had mentioned Ilford Wanders RFC and my Dad took me down a few times to play. I remember I actually played for Ilford Wanders against a team near where I lived in Epping. I made tackle after tackle at full back and surprisingly they had this big No.8 called Dean who just kept running into me one on one. He didn't try to side step I just went low and I seemed to take him down. Dad suggested I start playing for them. They were called Upper Clapton RFC and I spent the next 3 years as part of this local side. Steve Slade, who my dad had worked with at BT, coached us. Martin coached the forwards. Both of them top blokes who gave up time to train us and organise games at weekends for us.

All the boys from Upper Clapton RFC were from Epping or Harlow. I knew one guy lived down my road but most of them went to St John's, a school that seemed pretty rough and unsophisticated unlike mine that offered subjects like Latin and Ancient History. These lads could play rugby though and seemed a good bunch. I had had a few discos there when I met my friend, Tim Walker, and we used to go there dance, drink and chat up girls. My sister even had her 18th Birthday there and I remember driving home in my mum's Nissan Micro. I had to force her to pull over at the age of 15 as I was to be sick from the amount of alcohol I had consumed at the rugby club birthday party.

In the same year, we made the Middlesex cup final. I played full back and would love them to kick at me. I would usually kick back not very well but it was my job I guess to make territory even though maybe it was more of the case to not get tackled and hurt.

We had basic moves such as miss 1 play and scissors/pop from fly half to inside centre. We had a good kicker called Brian some pace on the wings. Robbie a hard centre and we had some big forwards like Deano and Adam Peeamamode.

I remember one game we played against Ilford Wanderers RFC who had a crazy player who started trying to punch our coach, Steve Slade. It was quite bizarre. Another game I scored a bunch of tries from the full back position. One guy who came with his dog kindly bought me a green polo shirt from the clubhouse shop with the clubs emblem and crest on the side.

We went to the final at Richmond RFC to play against Ruislip in the final. The pitch we played on was of a famous team although I hadn't realised it at the time. I didn't really touch the ball all game it was more done upfront. The ground was very dusty with hardly any grass on the surface. We had a very nice photo taken that was later sent to each player. It was 8-7 to us and they went to take a penalty and missed. We had a chance to make some points but decided to kick for the corner. Steve Slade was furious, as this could have cost us the game. We ended up holding them off and were crowned Middlesex Cup champions 1995-6. It was a great achievement even though we were a small club from the middle of nowhere in Essex.

Figure 5 Upper Clapton RFC 17th March 1996

We drove home singing rugby songs all the way with the old boys and very proud it was my first encounter with a true rugby social and loved the banter and singing.

Our end of season party was brilliant. Adam's parents ran the club bar Wendy and Ravi. We had a sponsor who looked after us. Mine was Tim Phelps' Dad who just laced and laced me with drinks. We had a big old meal and Deano and I nearly came to blows out the back at the golf driving range part of the club. We were both drunk while chuffing away on rolled up cigarettes. By 1998 I stopped playing for them as I went to University to do my HND in West Midlands.

Chapter 6

So after my A levels, I managed to get into a college to study an HND Higher National Diploma in Sound Engineering. The college was a few miles outside Birmingham but the halls of residence were at last 10 miles away. The actual campus didn't have a rugby team or any other recreational clubs. I'm sure it was limited due to the fact is was a sixth form college offering a handful of higher education and further education courses. I studied for a year and played for a local team in Wednesbury. We would play all around the East and West Midlands. I remember once stopping off from one pub to another and getting rather pickled. By the time we got back to our pokey little clubhouse, where there would usually be a big goat curry awaiting us to scoff, I would be struggling to keep up with the older guys. It was at Wednesbury RFC when I asked one lad to teach me to pour a pint. I wanted to get a job as a bartender on Birmingham's busy Broad Street and this was a perfect place to learn. No one was watching or judging and it wouldn't matter if I messed it up.

Around the spring of 1999 I was playing in one game against Bourneville from where the chocolate family originated. I felt really cold and tried the famous hands down the groin or under the armpit trick. The captain kept encouraging me to keep warm. That day I had ridden my bike down only a few miles from my halls of residence flat and when I got back to the clubhouse I felt weird and fatigued. I thought I better go home, leave the bike at the club, and get some rest. I was almost half tired half dizzy.

I slept from around 6 pm and woke up later drinking loads of orange juice. I slept all day the next day and started to have really bad diarrhoea. My housemates were asking if I wanted anything but I could barely answer. I asked them for a doctor on the Sunday but when they called the doctors they were closed or someone would tell them to send me down to the surgery the next day. I managed to get a taxi the next day. I knew something was wrong. I thought I just had a bug or tonsillitis, as my throat was now sore. I was aching and stiff all over and hallucinating while sleeping. I was in a bad state. I got to the busy Monday morning doctor's surgery and waited my turn. I was sprawled out along one of the benches to wake up to more people than I had originally remembered. Some how I realised I had had enough. I went to the toilet and just let my legs give way. I collapsed and it finally got their attention. I was rushed to a room. It looked like a kind of recovery ward and an ambulance was called. I would be in hospital for five days suffering blood poisoning a form of meningitis. I was pretty rough passing blood from my rear end and generally a very sick mess. I was hallucinating too and thought the cleaners were there to attack me. After being released from hospital I was told to get some TLC from my family. I went back to Essex. Dad pulled over at the services and I could barely walk or talk and just about managed it to the toilets. That weekend I was again taken back into hospital with pneumonia a double blow and ended up again in hospital for another week. Friends and family came to visit me of course and by the time I left I had lost a lot of weight almost 2 stone. I was to recover at home for a few more weeks before going back to study in Birmingham. I remember these horrible sickly sugary drinks I was told to drink to give me energy. Of course I did not play any more rugby for the rest of that season. I started going to the gym that May time and seemed to recover quite quickly. I was still skinny even after recovering and weighed just 11.5 stone. I went to the USA that summer to work on a summer camp in New York. I had also transferred to Salford University who worked along side my previous college. I transferred onto the Sound and Video Technology course that was split between the two institutions. I would be sure to check out the freshers' fair and join a rugby team when I arrived.

So September 1999 came around and I headed up to Manchester to the University of Salford. My Dad drove me up with all my stuff and I arrived late at the halls of residence called Churchill Court next to the Salford shopping precinct. That week I went to enrol and collect my student loan. I remember registering and seeing hundreds of hot girls from all backgrounds and races. Happy days I thought. I found my way to the fresher fair and had a nosey around campus, the sports hall and facilities. I went up to the rugby stand and met who turned out to be the captain, Richard Moorhouse. He was a hard looking northerner with short shaved ginger hair. He asked me if I was any good. I responded and said yes definitely. I think he warmed to my cockiness and he had a look in his eye that he trusted me.

We had freshers' trial. There was a lot of talent. I played pretty well. I remember I butchered a try the scrum half Stu Sorrel set me up with though. All I had to do was catch it and run it in. That didn't quite go to plan as I had white line fever. I was furious at myself as my hands were supposed to be a strong point of my game.

I remember an Irish man who kicked well. I also munched this guy with an England rugby jersey on. He wasn't too happy about that. This turned out to be Stu Barrett, a fun cocky lad. All in all it was a fun day. I think we had a freshers' pub crawl that night although I can't remember for sure. I do remember being at University House one time. Us Freshers were made to stand up in front of everyone including non-rugby drinkers in the student bar for what I learned to be a "Dip and down". Use your imagination for this one. This was a punishment of some kind although I was not aware of my crime. Slightly embarrassed I did mine and found it not as disgusting as I had first thought. Another initiation at a pub halfway from Castle Irwell to campus was a yard of Ale. I had never done one before although I had seen it. Around 3 pints took me 3 minutes to sink it was pretty hard work to do so from the gas if I remember. One lad, Zippy, took about 20 seconds...and with that gullet and mouth you can understand why his name was Zippy. He was named after the puppet from the kids programme "Rainbow" with a big mouth and a zip as lips.

Training was on Mondays and was taken by a man know as Bernie. He was an older northern man in his 50s. Stu would take a light training after game days on a Thursday. The training with Bernie was tough although it seemed quite basic. We had a horrible fitness Bernie would give us called Orrell bags, a tackling fitness exercise. You would tackle a man with a tackle shield then hit a long cylindrical tackle bag then return and hit the bag. It was very unpleasant. The other fitness we were given were the dreaded chain races. One person would start run out 40 meters and run back to get the second person. You both ran out and did the same to come and get the third person. And that was it. But then you would rotate. The guy that went last now went first and so on. So there would be three races in total all over within 10 minutes. Not a very nice experience I can tell you.

On fresher pub-crawl, I was talking and making new friends at the bars and pubs in Manchester. One lad who was nicknamed "Poo 2." I kept forgetting his name as we chatted and because I'd met and chatted to loads of the lads and the alcohol started kicking in I would ask him his name a few times. He then said I was similar to Trigger the character from the comedy "Only Fools and Horses" who always calls Rodney Trotter, "Dave". So my nickname was now "Trigger" meaning I was slightly stupid.

My first game against Hull we travelled for about two hours on the bus. I remember Richard's team talk to us. He said not to embarrass him in his backyard as he was from that area. I went on to score on my debut a very proud moment for me. It was Richard who inspired me to do my best for him and the team, as I didn't want to let him or anyone down. I played a couple of other first team games but then got dropped to the 2nd team that was captained by Rob Ladd. It was still a fun side and Rob was a fun captain. I was certain he was a nutter when it came to drinking. I saw him once drink 10 Reefs in 10 minutes. Reef was an alcoholic orange juice drink. I remember we went up to York and after scoring a few tries we walked back past the first team to watch the end of that game. Ben Cromey the fly half had been sick as soon as we dismounted the bus from too much booze from the night before. He then went on to kick the winning points from the touchline, a hard difficult kick that won Salford the game. The lads got the bus home but Phil Jarvis, another 2nd team comrade, and I stayed in York to visit my cousin and hit the town hard at nightclubs like Toffs, Ziggys and The Gallery. Another time we played University of Central Lancs in Preston. As a joke one of the lads said at the end of the game "Three cheers for Preston Poly…hip hip hurray" mocking their new University status. We went out in the town and one bar Tokyo Joes and The Varsity stand out in my mind. Two of the lads didn't make the 2 am bus that had waited to pick the team up and take us back to Salford. I wonder what they were doing?

I always seemed to get a mention in the student campus newspaper for scoring. They would always get my name wrong naming me "Dunsdeth", "Dunseth" or something similar. I piped up and corrected them. I then was given the nickname Dumnutz. This was certainly extremely annoying. I now had two bad nicknames for being stupid. "Trigger Dumnutz."

Other fresher's like Dino Markou reminded me of a Greek waiter, always in a newly pressed white shirt and black trousers. Stu Barrat would always make up lies inviting Ben Cromey and me to drive in his dads Rover to Cream the nightclub as he had tickets. He also claimed he had played cricket for England schools and had joined the Royal Air force. Apparently his father worked for the Daily Mail newspaper and lived in New Zealand. Stu seemed to tell a bunch of other general pork pies.

Ben Cromey turned out to be a bit feisty. He had another friend who both lived on campus. Ben came home once slightly intoxicated and urinated in someone's spaghetti bolognese into someone's utterly butterly, butter as a joke. But the prank backfired. He was called to the accommodation office and he and Bianca were split up and moved in to different houses on campus. Extremely foul but immensely funny in my opinion. Another time Ben and Kev Rogers Davidson were in the Pav. A waitress came round with two burger and chips and asked who had ordered the delicious dishes. Ben and Kev announced they had and quickly devoured the two portions. The problem was that they hadn't ordered or paid for them. The security marched over and demanded to see their student cards. They were reported to campus admin and almost banned from the student facilities. In my opinion, it was a very funny prank and the punishment was far too much. Taking away a rugby player's privilege to attend events at the Pav was extreme totalitarian. But this is what the rugby lads did. Rather obnoxious behaviour occurred when we got together. But we were all mates and had a laugh as a group. It was almost like a brotherhood. Dave Rotherham once downed a bottle of red wine and ran naked around the cricket pitch. He took his punishments well and received a standing ovation. I don't really remember any fighting though. Maybe everyone was scared of us or maybe they knew we were too drunk but I'm sure we annoyed a few people either in the Pav or elsewhere. When there was "Man of the Match" and "Cunt of the Match" (this was the person who played badly or did something outrageously stupid during the game) a sick bucket was always brought out by Mike the guy who ran the student bar. We were made to do "dip and downs" in the Pav, too, in front of the rest of the students whoever happened to be there at the time. A boat race was always a good shout against the opposition and I soon joined the team for the small drinking abilities I had. Zippy was an obvious team player, usually going last to finish the job off to secure victory.

As stated he had been given this title after the children's programme "Rainbow" as he could open his mouth and lose his drink in seconds referring to the character Zippy with a rather large gob. Everyone needed a Zippy on their drinking team.

Bernie would come for a drink sometimes after the game but not often. He was a nice guy and was quite witty. Named the "BPS" The Blackpool Shagger. Once I was being smart about a girl that had taken my eye. He said I was young and naive and he knew more about what the ladies wanted. I asked him how. He said, "I was a young bull and he was an old bull" Then he proceeded to tell me a story. "The young bull said 'Dad! Dad! Lets run down the hill and fuck a cow' The old bull said, 'No son lets stroll down and fuck all of them'." Good advice from a man that knew.

It was funny. One of the rugby guys in the Pav asked me where I was from. I told him a small town in Essex. He obviously knew I was from down south from my accent. He was called Owen Evans who soon went on to have a very funny nickname. He also happened to be from Epping the same small town as myself. It's a small world indeed as they say.

I was only at Salford until the end of January until I moved back to Birmingham due to the course being split between the two institutions.

I missed the lads instantly. I remember being sad and begged my Dad to let me move back and commute from Manchester. It was a ridiculous request but I remember missing my non-rugby friends too. I remember the conversation on the phone to Ben and telling him I hated leaving Salford.

That's spring though I would go back a bit to visit friends and have fun in Manchester. I would see Josh and Matt the American lads. We would hang out at the gym and in the night go out partying. The other rugby lads said Matt and Josh danced like MC Hammer. I would meet up with Jarvis and Ben and we would go to the Pav the student bar/nightclub on Castle Irwell campus. We would go to other cheap places in Manchester usually places that did special drink deals where it would be £1 a pint.

I started work at Sports Café in Birmingham. I told my mother about the up and coming rugby tour. She felt it wouldn't be fair if I were to be the only one not to go. I think she sent me a cheque or something and it paid for the flight and hotel. The tour was to the cheap British holiday destination of Benidorm and we were to fly into Alicante. We all dyed our hair Blue and Yellow after the Salford shirt colours. Mine went a sort of gingery blond colour, which almost made me look like a poor version of Eminem the rapper "Slim Shady". Once out there the tour was pretty messy. There were two hotels. I shared a room with Ben Cromey, Ryan Watson the big no.8 and "Action" otherwise known as Michel Clark. He was known as Action as he was a bit of a militant with certain types of artillery mostly illegal no doubt. The room became a zoo and Ben instantly smashed a glass and left all the broken pieces on the floor. Ryan and Ben had also claimed the beds. I was made to sleep on the sofa bed with Action. Oh the joy of that!

We had a few nights out and Ben myself and Ryan broke away from the main older group who tried to rule over us. We used to drink either down at the beach or up on the roof top pool deck. The litre bottles of San Miguel cost a few Euros each. It was good fun hanging out with the two lads and plenty of banter was had. Foxy, who played full back, had his eyebrows shaved off in the night. While he had passed out, one of the lads took a razor as a practical joke. Apparently he had a job interview the following week and was so angry that he declared himself "Off Tour". He wore his sunglasses all week and sulked on his own.

There was one German tourist lady who didn't like us too much and we called her Mole. One great quote from her was "Ahhhh so that's where you have been hiding." Then there was the

Dutch guy who we would bump into at the swimming pool who loved "Manchester United". He looked like the BFG, lanky with big ears. Ben made good friends by banging on people's doors at 4 am. It was his morning rendition of "Knock Down Ginger." Of course one guy answered by coming out wearing nothing but his white briefs and yelled at Ben inN some sort of European language, probably to kindly "Fuck Off". Ben would yell back at them something just as pleasant. Kev regarded his manhood as the "General" that spoke French and the DJ didn't quite understand who exactly the General was. The phrase "Talking Willy" was introduced. Ben and I invented two imaginary rugby players called Steve and Neil to confuse the older players when brought into the conversation. They would stand clueless wondering who these two players were as we both kept straight faces.

On the way home one night Owen Evans allegedly was taking a local girl with him. I wasn't there but the rumour has it that some local lads, who were jealous of an Englishman taking one of their girls, confronted him. Apparently the rumour says, that Owen, who was quite non-confrontational, excreted in his pants earning himself the title of "Shitty Pants."

We played Freshers v Old boys someway out of the town but apart from that that was the only rugby I played.

At University previously that year I met a Spanish girl through my French housemates. We would sometimes go out as a group, our flat and theirs, that was in the sister tower block next to ours. One of the girls, Marta, had gone back to Tarragona in Spain. She had been an exchange student studying briefly at Salford University. I really liked her and decided to go up and visit. I would take the six-hour bus journey up and bring her some perfume as a gift. I went out the night before to a big nightclub with Dino, Ben, Action and Ryan. I was pretty intimidated by the place. The size of the place, the music and the type of people to me was scary. I left around 5-6 am and the sun was coming

66

up. I set my alarm and asked Action to wake me up to get my early bus. You guessed it; I missed it and as I was on such a strict budget had to buy a new ticket. I was gutted and my heart sank. I really wanted to see Marta. She was after all very beautiful. All the lads ribbed and made fun of me. Sure enough someone lent me the money to get another ticket. I travelled up, met Marta, arriving late evening. She took me to a tapas bar. There we eat solidified pig's blood like English black pudding. We went to another place and we had a dance and a few Ballentine whiskeys. She showed me her work place and I remember the town being very pretty and old. Nothing happened between Marta and I. We didn't even kiss but I'm glad I went up to see her. On the way back on the bus I passed through Denia, Castillo and Valencia so at least I saw a bit of Spain. Some local girls gave me some sunflower seeds and we shared Spanish Fortuna cigarettes on the back of the bus. I arrived back and the lads had played a game against Hull University in my absence. They still couldn't believe I had left the rugby team to drive halfway across Spain to see a girl. We all flew home quite tired but we had all had had a fun trip. Some of the lads had taken Owen aka "Shitty Pant's" debit card and were exploiting copious amounts of drinks on the airline, without him knowing. I got back to Manchester, stayed at my mate's house for a bit at Waterside Student Village to recuperate and then made my way back to Birmingham. I arrived and couldn't find my keys, which was a pain. I found out sometime later that the boys had stolen them as a joke. Luckily I was able to get my housemates to let me in. I got my pictures developed from my Kodak ADVANTIX camera I had bought the previous summer in the USA. I had had a lot of fun memories of the tour all of us drinking having fun with our dyed yellow hair.

I came back to Birmingham and didn't play any rugby for Wednesbury. I lived far away and worked most weekends in the bar until the late hours anyway.

Figure 6 Salford University rugby tour to Spain 2000

Chapter 7

That summer I reapplied for my American J1 Visa to go back and work on the summer camp in New York. My visa application arrived back late so I had to change my flight a week later costing a fair amount more. I spent six weeks with my friend Tim from Essex who was also on the trans-Atlantic programme and after the camp ended, I stayed in New York with Tim partying and having fun. I emailed a team in New York called Old Blue RFC. They trained on Randall's Island, an old disused dumping ground off Manhattan. I went to training and the team seemed like a good standard. I would be second team standard. They promised me a place to stay and a job. I was staying in hostels with Tim and my money was starting to wear thin. I was not very financially responsible throughout my twenties. My motto was to have fun now pay later and worry about how I'd pay for things when the problem arose. There was actually one guy from my University called Dempsey playing for Old Blue. I had never met him but it was a small world. I tried getting a job everywhere as a bartender but I got the usual answer, no. Unless I had a social security number people would not hire me. The rugby guys put me onto some construction company based north of NY outside a place called Yonkers. Once I touched base with them I would be asked to go to Staten Island, one of the five boroughs that make up New York City. They wanted me there for 8 am. One of the guys I would be working with would pick me up. I was staying in Chelsea a Manhattan neighbourhood. I would get the subway down to the Wall Street area and Battery Park to get the free Staten Island ferry over. It was nice and cool in the mornings especially going over the water. The guys I worked with were great fun all Irish American fire fighters earning an extra dollar on their days off. We were decorating a school and I was just a general dogsbody. The days went quickly and they would end the day with a few beers. The guy in charge always bumped my hours up slightly to help me out if I was late or we finished early. They were my kind of people.

One day though I went to training on Randall's Island and no one was there. I wasted two hours getting there via Malcolm X Boulevard, a pretty rough neighbourhood past uptown Manhattan. I was pretty angry no one had informed me about the change of location for training so I gave my point of contact from the rugby team a phone call. His wife or girlfriend answered and I told her to pass on "a not so pleasant have a nice day message" to her male counterpart from the team. The next day I received a stinking email from him telling me they only wanted thick-skinned players in their team. I didn't return to play so I looked around for other teams. I found one called Long Island RFC. It was based outside Manhattan a train ride away. I would meet the captain, Scott, who turned out to be the biggest player I have ever met. He was a prop of course and picked me up from somewhere in the borough of Queens. Tim my mate from the UK had flown back to London and I was still trying to live the dream in New York. I moved up to Spanish Harlem for about five days at around $30 a night in a hostel. The training went well and we had a 10-minute run around the pitch to warm up. I wanted to show my fitness and bombed off to the front. I wore my favourite Fiji shirt to stand out.

John coached them. He had white hair and also worked in the TV/Audio business. He smoked cigars at training. Another coach was Mac, a huge tall stocky Kiwi who was a security guard at the UN building in Manhattan. I was asked what I was doing that weekend. They had a game in Danbury, Connecticut and a stag party was being thrown after. I was eager to play. The guys seemed friendly and a good standard and they wanted me at full back. I decided to go and was very excited. We played the game and I scored on my debut. A great feeling as Mike the Kiwi fly half floated the ball out to me to race over the line.

The stag party was great. It was John Ashcare's. I hung out with Bill Callaghan the inside centre they called IDK because he always said, "I don't know", Jerry McCarthy the feisty scrum half from Philadelphia who they called Pennsylvania pain, and Kevin Carbina. All the guys were in the mid to early 30s. It was a great stag party, my first in fact. There was illegal gambling and betting and I some how won four tickets to the Yankees baseball game the next day. Kevin was a massive Yankees fan and jumped on me to go. He said he would take me and invite his friend. We could also sell a ticket for extra beer money. It sounded like a good plan to me. That night of the party the lads smuggled me into my first strip club, even though I was only 20. I was never short of a beer and was given some funny money for a lap dance.

The next day we drove back and sure enough me and Kevin met his friend and we went to the baseball drank more and nurtured our hangovers.

I went back to my hostel where I had left my suitcase and stuff for the last two days. Everything was intact and untouched, surprisingly. The following few days Jerry said I could stay with him at his house in Long Island. I took the train to 34th Street Penn station. I had worked there a few weeks previously handing out the Daily News Express, a free paper. However I never got paid as I didn't have a social security number and couldn't fulfil the requirements for banking and tax on the forms I was asked to fill out after doing a day's work.

I went to Long Island and ended up meeting Jerry. Jerry owned a franchise in a company called Dent Wizard. He had acquired the skills to knock out dents in cars after small collisions or scrapes. He had earned some money in the construction industry and now did something a bit different. Jerry was fun. He was a good player on the field and enjoyed partying. He was 34 years old and seemed to be in his element. That week he said I could stay on his couch. He told me to take his bike up to the

Huntingdon Golf club and get a job as a caddy. He had a nice girlfriend at the time called Kate. She was really nice but I was very intimidated around her as she was so fit. She invited me to an 80's nightclub in Manhattan some time later. I was petrified she was going to make a pass on me. Jerry had been kind and like a fun big brother to me. He had taken me into his house. I remember him saying "Take this $100 you will need it, you always need money in your back pocket". I went to the golf club and met another English guy, older, in his late 40's. He sounded from his story as though he was on the run from the UK and explained to me various tax scams he knew. I told them Jerry was my cousin in case they were going to be nosey about my working papers. The head caddy gave me a shot and I started carrying golf bags around the course for $80 a bag, some days carrying two golf bags and going the course twice. I found it pretty tough. Worse still I had broken a finger from training. Every time I shook hands with someone it was painful as hell. I remember losing one doctor's putter. If they asked for advice I would tell them what they wanted to hear regarding what club to use and how far the pin was. To be honest I had no idea.

The weather wasn't great and with rain (work on the course became slow) I decided to get a second job working in a bagel store on Main Street of the town. We played rugby each week in Bayonne, Montclair, and we even went out to play near Montauk in the Hamptons on Long Island where you would see the odd windmill here and there, probably influenced by the early Dutch settlers.

I would score usually each game and enjoyed the rugby very much with the team. Jerry took me to Philadelphia. We watched the baseball there and then partied on South Street at the bars. Again Jerry had to smuggle me in as I was still under the drinking age of 21.

My time in New York was coming to an end. The boss at the bagel store was getting annoyed as I didn't want to work

Saturdays and this was his busiest day. I was playing rugby and having too much fun. I had moved in with Jenn above Jerry. She happened to be the same age as him and was blind. She could navigate around her flat though and used to walk in while I was taking a bath. It felt weird having her talking to me but not being able to see anything. One night we went out. She got far too drunk and I had to carry her into the taxi and get her up the stairs at the house to the flat we stayed in.

I did a few other casual jobs but the season was coming to an end of what proved to be a mild autumn for New York. I raked leaves and got another two days a week job at a deli serving coffees, sandwiches, cold cut meats and cheeses. I had left the bagel store. The boss accused me of stealing money from the till or giving too much change to customers. I felt this was really unfair, as I never stole any money. I did however help myself to the Nesquik milk and Snapple juices. I would toss the bottles over the fence to a waste ground to get rid of the evidence.

On my last day in New York I did some dry wall plaster boarding for one of the players, Todd. I was his assistant and after around 4 pm I would race to the Irish pub to have my leaving party. I had no mobile but I ended up being at least two and a half hours late. The trains were running slow and I eventually made it. Doctor Keith bought me a shot of whiskey and left due to having family commitments. IDK or Bill led us all down stairs to a room lined with chairs in a semi circle. I had no idea what was happening. We were then presented with complimentary dollars and in walked an absolute stunning lady with huge boobs. She introduced herself as "Coco Chanel". They had hired a stripper for me and a sex show was about to commence. I was embarrassed as hell and told to strip to my boxers. I wore some rag tag wholly horrible green Marks & Spencers torn and ripped boxer shorts. The lady stripped and she presented me with a dildo. I had no idea what the rabbit ears did and or what a clit was when she asked me to play with it. All the lads laughed their heads off. I thought it was to be inserted into her anus. Jerry was urging me on and it just embarrassed me further. How wrong could I be? Coco needed a volunteer and Berdie quickly offered his services to her who kindly accepted graciously. Berdie was now on nipple duty and he would tweak them whilst sat behind her. The party ended and we all had a great night thanks to IDK who arranged everything. The lads presented me with a framed photo of myself at full pace stiff-arming a player from the opposition. It had a caption saying, "Liam you always have a home in New York" A nice gesture I was sure to treasure and cherish. The lads were always fun. They were so welcoming. They enjoyed life and rugby. I wanted to go back to New York but I decided I should return to the UK to finish off my HND. So that November of 2000 I flew home.

LIRFC v. Montauk 10/31/00

Liam- You always have a home in New York. Well played. LIRFC

Figure 7 Playing my last game in Long Island, New York

Chapter 8

I stayed at my Dad's for a few weeks until I had earned enough money from window cleaning for Alex Coker's dad to go back to Salford and finish off my studies. The modules were a couple of hundred pounds so I used the money from an overdraft to fund it. I started working at Loaf nightclub bar on Deansgate Locks and my mate Phil Jarvis let me crash at his house for a bit on Seaford Road, a notorious hot spot for scallys. Phil and I had a fight as I went too far with a joke throwing him into the street naked with a towel wrapped round him. I thought it was funny but he was unimpressed.

Ben Cromey was living with "Action" and Jamie not too far away and they told me to come round with my stuff. I only had a suitcase so it was fine. I arrived at Wellington Street West. This was up the hill toward Cheatham, a run down area and extremely working class, like much of Salford. The place was a shit tip but living with rugby lads would be fun. Plus it was free, as the landlord didn't know I was there.

I would sometimes get home from working at 3-4 am from the bar after cleaning up. The next day I would then play rugby at Trafford MV an old school rugby club near Sale and Stretford. The playing ground was like a farmer's paddock and the changing rooms were almost like a cattle shed but the coach Bernie would look after us. Rob Ladd would be scrum half, Cromey at fly half, myself and Jarvis on the wings etc Zippy and Big Kev in the forwards. Wilf would hog the ball, as he wasn't too happy about us students scoring all the points. I would go to work in the evening. Later on when we went on University road trips against the away teams we would make prank telephone calls pretending it was Manchester police and that we had Wilf's missing shoe. We informed him he needed to come down with two forms of identification to pick up his shoe. His response was "Which one of you students is it this time?"

We had a rugby tournament down at Keele University. We had the first and second team players one Sunday afternoon. The bus took us all down very early to their campus. I vaguely remember it being a sort of 10's tournament. However we arrived around 10.30 am and the bus left in agreement to pick us up at 6 pm. We checked in and it was revealed that the pitches had frozen over. Well we were stranded what else could we do. So we started drinking pints of famous "Diesel" a blend of cider, lager and blackcurrant otherwise known as "Snakebite and Black". A court session occurred. I was fined for something naughty. Alex Cosgrove and me had to strip naked, hold hands and run round the car park as our fine. "BigShow" was also fined. He would have to lift himself on his hands while two players held his legs in the air. A pint was poured down the crack on his arse and the liquid was caught in his muddy boot. He would then have to drink from the boot for his heinous crime. This to my recollection was the worst punishment a player received. Luckily, I never had to do it. Arriving back to the group we had to down a pint of Diesel with Baileys, red wine, rice and Tabasco. We continued to drink all day. People talk about peer pressure but this was different. You just accepted it and went with the flow regardless. A few Baileys were sunk. On the bus home finally when we left around 5-6 pm I was a bit worse for wear and vomited. No one wanted to sit next to me for obvious reasons.

In the spring of 2001 the Six Nations rugby had started. Somehow the University was allocated tickets that could be purchased from the RFU ticketing board for the games. We all decided to go down to London for the England v Italy game. I had been working at Loaf on Deansgate Locks until 3 am. I got home and stayed up for a bit then it was time to leave and get to Manchester Piccadilly for the 7 am train. I think a few of the lads had done the same and stayed up all night except they had been boozing. I had been on my feet all night serving pissed up

Manchurians beers, shot and whatever else they had been yelling at me for. Some of us went to the greasy spoon café for a breakfast and coffee. Some how through the student travel agency, we had been given first class tickets to London for £10. We took over the carriage completely, drinking cans of beer and singing. The dress code was shirts and skirts. This consisted of a rugby shirt and a female skirt. Some borrowed from housemates, some borrowed of their girlfriends but to be honest I didn't know too many girls to ask this sort of favour. Also it was not really my thing but I stood out for not wearing the correct attire. The funny thing was several months later a guy came up to me while I was pouring pints at Loaf and said, "I recognise you...you dress up in a skirt" I had no idea what he was talking about. He then went on to say that he was from London but lived up here and he was going back down south to watch the Tottenham game. The fact that he recognised me from the train that day was rather funny, even though I hadn't been wearing one of these ludicrous outfits that the rest of the lads had.

Around Christmas 2000, my friend Jim from the summer camp who lived in New York asked me if I wanted to go on spring break in Florida. We had kept in contact via email. I had never been to Florida and wanted to go. I had not heard of spring break but he explained in Daytona Beach, it was warm, the girls were crazy and always up for partying. I spoke to my friend Ben Mosquera who was working in a dead end job at the time. He had finished his Master's degree and was not sure what he wanted to do. I explained that if we flew to New York we would meet my friend Jim, get a greyhound bus down to Florida, and get a motel then party. From there we could go back to New York get a job in the construction company and live there too. Plus I'd be able to play rugby for Long Island again. It sounded like a foolproof plan. Ben would be saving during the next three months. I would be spending and partying. Come March the rugby boys prank called me and said it was the landlord and that

I owed a certain amount of money for staying at Wellington Street West. They texted me saying it was Terry Ryan who was actually our landlord and that if I tried to leave the country he would have me arrested at the airport. I fell for it obviously. I think even Ben was surprised how gullible I was at biting the bait. Shitting myself, I packed all my stuff into boxes and a suitcase and legged it to Chinese "Mickey's" who was a winger from the second team. He lived around the corner and I made my get away. I told the landlord I would wire it from N-Y-C. "Yer, right" I thought, there's no chance of that happening pal. Johnny Sadler, Cromey and Jamie were all in stitches pissing themselves laughing. I then moved my stuff from Chinese Mikey's to Ben's mum and dad's house in Heywood north of Manchester in Lancashire.

Chapter 9

Ben and I booked our flights with Air Canada to New York via Toronto for £230. We got to Port Authority in Manhattan and bought our bus tickets except I only had enough money for a single to Daytona. We boarded the greyhound bus with Jim and off we set. It was good fun. I had no idea what I was in for. I was more worried that I had no cash. My visa electron card would not give me any money. I was supposed to have been paid in the UK the day before and for some reason I couldn't take any money out. I only had about $40. I tried selling my passport to whoever looked dodgy at the bus terminal. It's crazy to think back now. We made friends with some young ladies on the bus and I remember waking up to warm sunshine about two hours north of our destination. We arrived around 9 am and we took a taxi to our motel. After a week of partying Ben and I spoke about maybe staying in Daytona rather than going back to New York. I finally had money wired from my Abbey National bank account and Tim Walker's dad sent me some money too. Ben managed to find us a place to stay with a man at the local biker bar. He wanted to sublet his basement. It had a double bed, stone concrete floors and a weird bathroom. We would both pay $80 a week but get the run of the house when the guy went to work during the day. It was a great deal. The house was built on the sand dunes so a perfect spot and location for sunbathing and beach access. We went looking for work too and after draping around Daytona begging people one lady from the Italian restaurant told us to come back the next day. When we did, she offered us jobs as waiters. The place was called Palermo's. It was brilliant. We celebrated hard. That week we had gone out to use Internet café and bought French fries and a coke in exchange for the use of the computers and Internet. The library was across the International Bridge but this was easier. I went on Yahoo and, to my amazement and happiness, I found a local rugby team. They were associated with the Aeronautical University

Embry Riddle, some four miles inland. I decided to go and find them and see if I could train. I called one guy who sounded very much English. He was Kenyan and called Robin Bairstow. I went to gather my boots and started walking from the library. I walked down International Speedway Boulevard thinking it would only take me about 45 minutes. It started taking a while and when I asked a local he told me to go left. I started walking and suddenly realised when I came to an old liquor store - it looked like one from the 80s movies - very eerie looking with ethnic minorities gathering around outside. From the look of the local houses, too, this didn't seem a very good neighbourhood. Nothing happened to me and no one approached me but I was slightly alarmed. A cop car pulled up and I said I was lost. They seemed concerned about who had sent me down here when I had asked where the Embry Riddle playing fields were. I thought they might give me a lift but for me no such luck. I continued to walk and a few minutes later a car pulled over it was a bunch of rugby lads. Robin the white Kenyan I had spoke to and Gabe a mixed race Canadian guy. They took me to the playing fields. The training however had changed location to the police baseball field so even if I had found the University playing fields I would have gone to the wrong place. Was this fate of some kind I thought? Here I met a bunch of guys mostly students training to be pilots. That week I was supposed to go to Tampa with the rugby team as Steve one of the Kenyan students had injured his leg quite badly and they needed a full back. I had celebrated the night before from partying knowing Ben and I were going to be staying and living in Daytona. The next day, I didn't make it up in time and had no idea who to call or where to meet. That night Ben and I went over to the mainland to a place called Love and Groove bar. There I bumped into Doc and Gab. Doc's real name was James Brown but everyone called him Doc for obvious reasons. Doc was short and stocky very strong and quick. We were about the same speed. Doc was doing his residency at the local Halifax hospital after med school in

Tampa. He had played rugby for about six years and wrestled too in college. Gab was a big strong Canadian with a big grin. I think he played prop. They were surprised to see me there as I was due to play and I felt pretty bad bailing on them but I explained the reason. They said I was lucky to have bumped into them as they were going to party down in Tampa but had decided to come back to Daytona, as it was St Patrick's Day. The bar we were in was called "Love" and the nightclub next door was called "Groove." There was also a restaurant called "Mongolian Grill" and the guy called Milthouse owned all three. That night, before I met up with Gabe and Doc, I told the guy on the door that I washed pots for Milthouse in the kitchen and to let me in for free as I was staff. He obliged kindly. Ben and I had previously been for a job interview and it looked like Milthouse was going to give us jobs so I used that to my advantage. I had a lot of fun and it was a good night. The following week I tried the same stunt and my blag was sussed by the guy who said he hadn't seen me about; I got away with it though not sure how.

That week Ben and I were working in the restaurant. Our living arrangements were starting to take their toll because we shared a double bed and being around each other each day. I had also not paid Ben's mum back the rest of the flight money and nerves were getting tense between us.

I took off the Tuesdays and Wednesdays from work for training and one night at the police baseball field there was a short water break. Abraham and I carried on while everyone quenched their thirst and decided to kick some "up and under's" to each other. Except on one of the kicks we both went up for it as it descended. I found myself on the floor not knowing what had happened. Blood gushed from my right eyebrow and its safe to say I had no idea how it had happened. I could only guess it was his knee, elbow or head that I had made contact with, to split open my eyebrow. No one seemed to be that bothered but the blood was pretty dark and everyone else seemed to carry on regardless. Even Doc had a quick look and was a bit unsure which wasn't that reassuring to me considering he was supposed to be a doctor. Andy, who was from Ohio and doing an internship for NASCAR said I better go to hospital and have it checked out. We drove there about 10-15 minutes away and somehow I stopped it from bleeding. I was pretty worried, as I had no medical insurance coverage. I was extremely carefree back then and took those kind of irresponsible risks by not worrying about things like that. We arrived and the nurse looked at me once they made me fill out the paperwork etc and billing to the UK. Andy asked, "Will you staple it or stitch it?" Thanks mate that's just what I wanted to hear. Sure enough though it did need stitches. Four of the stitches apparently dissolved into the skin and tissue and eight external ones that would need to be taken out the following week. Andy took me back to Palermo's the Italian restaurant. Ben didn't seem too bothered. Well why would he, it wasn't his fault, but Agi the lady in charge our boss was very motherly and probably gave Andy and myself some free food. Of course I had no intention of going back to have my stitches out. I didn't want another bill coming my way. It was probably free but I thought it be best to stay away from the hospital under the circumstances. I managed to cut the stitches myself the next week and pull them out. It wasn't easy and I kept finding bits of plastic thread in my eyebrow, poking out in days to come. Andy would later go on to call me "The Ram" as I would duck my head into the tackle apparently like a ram does with his horns in battle. That weekend we were to play in the Florida finals playoffs. We would play against Naples a strong team. We drove to Orlando. I think I was a sub and I came on as a flanker. I have never been a strong aggressive tackler but somehow I tackled my heart out. Andy was playing scrum half and we had the usual Kenyans like Jazzy Jeff, Abraham and other classic players like Doc, Gary Wolyzan, Grabo and his son. We got completely smashed and they scored about seven tries to one. It was slightly embarrassing and a bit of an anti climax to be honest against a tough team. That was now it for the rest of the 15's season.

Around this time I made friends with an Irish lad also training to be a pilot who was from Galway. He was three to four years older than me like Andy and Ben. His name was John Ellard and instead of training at Embry Riddle like the other student pilots he was based at Phoenix flying school next to Daytona International Airport. John had got injured some weeks before I had arrived and Robin, due to the many injuries John suffered, gave him the title "Band-Aid", the American name for plaster. We would all go to the Irish pub Robbie O' Connell's. There Ben, Andy, John and I would drink before going to Razzles nightclub or 600 North. Typically on Wednesdays we would go to Razzles for ladies night in Daytona and on a Thursday, Doc and Carlos would come to 600 North. We would get in for free and I would blag my way in via the manager Joe Victorelli. This was because the rugby team had done some volunteer work during spring break and Joe rewarded us by giving us free entry. Either that or he was just not bothered about locals paying. At Razzles, I would have a fake ID as I was still under 21 and I would give the spiel that I was a student at Embry Riddle. So I was classed as a local and they waved the cover entrance charge. It seemed to work all the time. 600 North would have 25-cent drafts of some cheap beer like Bud light or Coors light and a Venus swimwear contest on Thursdays. We all loved Jessica, Joe's wife, and two other smoking hot bartenders, Tara and Angela, both probably having fake boobs. I would go in with $15 and come out with change, it was that cheap. I remember Doc, Carlos, Band-Aid and myself buying 16 small beers about a pint each and it came to $4.

The 7s season would start around April/May and we would train every Tuesday and Thursday at Embry Riddle playing fields that backed onto Clyde Morris and International Speedway Boulevard.

In the May, I met a wonderful girl in a bar one night out with Andy. She was with her friend. Both were called Carrie. We all went to the Ocean Deck beach bar and met them randomly. I tried enticing them to Razzles nightclub and Andy suggested strongly we go swimming and even better skinny-dipping. We played about in the water and later on bother decided to swap girls. I was now with the lovely blond and Andy with the brunette. We stayed the night in their time-share condo. That next day Andy was to pack up as his internship was over with NASCAR. I was really sad and gave him my Wellington Hurricanes rugby shirt, which, incidentally, I have never seen him wear. It was my favourite shirt and I wouldn't mind it back actually.

Come June time, Ben's tourist visas and mine were coming to an end. I was supposed to go up to New York but had stayed in Daytona. Another girl had asked me to her high school prom; although she was 18 the two-year age different wasn't a big deal to me but I never made the move up north, probably because I was having so much fun in Daytona playing rugby and partying.

We played at St Petersburg near Tampa and had one guy, Abel, a skinny but ripped Puerto Rican guy on our team. He was very cocky and funny. Suspicion was that he was on steroids and slightly gay. He was great chatting to the ladies with a body of a god. It was just a shame for the ladies he had big ears and goofy teeth. For us though this didn't matter. Abel had played American football in high school and was really quick. He was a character and didn't really know the game at all but he knew how to run. At the St Pete tournament he would run in about 8 tries. We got to the final and unfortunately lost. I remember the look of disappointment on Doc's face and vowed never to be in that situation again. It was heart breaking. We had left earlier in convoy from Daytona with seven players. Abraham had to leave early to get back for work in Daytona. We picked up another player, Mike, from Brevard, a Kiwi guy who was a pretty useful player. I scored a few tries that day and got sin binned after one guy had high tackled me and I reacted stupidly. Abel came to my rescue and floored the guy but I was pinged for it even after scoring, I was yellow carded. We lost in a game later in the final but we were all pretty chuffed. Jazzy Jeff, Iowa, Lee from Argentina, Doc, Abel, Band-Aid and myself all had a fun day and went back to Daytona rather pleased with what we had achieved. That June I had my 21st birthday and we all partied hard. I remember Gary Wolyzen and Carlos coming to my birthday in Razzles on the Tuesday night; it was dead. I took my passport and the guy on the day was shocked to see I was 21 that day and had been coming for a few months. Gary took me to Lollipops and handed me a bunch of singles. I was pretty drunk and he told me to enjoy myself but it had been enough for him and he was leaving. I laughed as I watched him stagger drunk out of the strip club.

A few months before, I moved from the garage to the room next to it attached to the house, to what could only be called, a broom cupboard/junk room. The door was falling off and certainly had no lock on it. It was filled with suitcases, kids toys and I managed to make a bed out of a type of chaise long and a big plastic container turned upside down. But after a few months it had become a bit too much of squalor for me.

By the end of June, I ended up moving in with John aka Band-Aid. He lived in a nice apartment mainland. I would buy a bike from the second-hand store and bike to and from work. Sometimes John would take the bike in his jeep and drop me off in Daytona Beach Shore to the restaurant and I would just bike it back. He didn't charge me rent which was really nice and had Internet too. It was also nice, clean and cool with air conditioning.

We also played in the Todd Miller tournament in Orlando although we lost most games and didn't do too well. The Todd Miller tournament was dedicated to a young man who unfortunately lost his life after an accident in a scrum leaving him severely damaged. I remember making a break and Robin screaming at me to keep going and not to look round as to who was chasing me. Jim Smorto would come and film the games on his Hi-8 or Docs old school SVHS camera. It was a great summer of 7s but by the time August had come around the tournaments had dried up and I was ready to go back to the UK. I decided to fly up to Ohio to see Andy. That summer I had met a few girls who lived in Cleveland, Ohio and I thought if I flew to see Andy maybe we could make a road trip out of it. This is what I did. So I booked a cheap Airtran ticket. Lee or as he was known as "Argentina", because he was from there surprisingly enough, drove me to the airport. I gave him $10 for gas and my rugby ball. I arrived late and I spent one night in the town Andy had grown up in and then in the morning we set off to Cleveland. Andy had a female friend he said we could stay with which was ideal. We all went out with Erin and her friends from John Carrol University in Cleveland and Erin was very kind to me. We got quite friendly and she invited me to hang out with her and her friends once the bars closed. Andy went to stay with Ashley and Erin kindly asked me to spend the rest of the night or morning as it was with her. A few days later I took a greyhound bus to New York. I arrived very late after about 12 hours and took the Long Island railroad to Huntington, something I had done a few times the previous year. Jerry picked me up and drove us to his house. He had moved out of the split-level house where he had lived downstairs and me upstairs with Jenn the blind lady. He was now renovating a house of his own. I helped dig foundation and shift rocks. He had a bunch of dirty manual labour jobs for me and as I needed the pocket money; it was ideal seeing as he would have employed a labourer anyway. It was a big old house and he had gutted it completely living upstairs while the downstairs was being knocked out and rebuilt. It was an eyesore from the street and generated a lot of interest from neighbours.

I stayed with Jerry for a few days and I would speak with Erin a few times on the phone before leaving to go back to the UK.

Chapter 10

I flew back to the UK and it was my Dads 50th Birthday. He had the party at the bar of Old Brentwoods' rugby club. I had played a few games for the lads at Old Brentwoods' RFC when I was back from University and staying back in Essex. At the club, they had tennis courts cricket and football pitches but the main emphasis was the rugby. Dad got involved through Ann, his partner, and it was Ann's friend, Maggie, who was married to Tim Faires, the President of the rugby club who encouraged my Dad to bring me along. I would play for the second team with the likes of Neil Tetner, an ex Upper Clapton lad, a bit older than me, Billy a big Pacific Islander who played no.8 and the Hannaway brothers Ian and Neil, known as "Fat boy" and "Ginga." I would play full back or one of the wingers as I had some speed and the games were generally easy for me running past the old men who we had as opposition. The lads treated me well and looked after me. That time of year before I went back to University, I played for Old Bs and "Ginga" started playing me at fly half. It was a difficult position and he explained a few fundamental things about positioning myself as a fly half to where the scrum half would be to pass. He would encourage me and talk to me throughout the game and if I made a mistake or a bad decision he would gee me up. He gave me confidence to forget it and move on. He was a nice bloke and told me it was not an easy position to master. Nav, one of the flankers who was a bit younger than me, would kindly drive to Epping to pick me up. Epping was about 12 miles from the rugby club. Also a good bloke, Nav later moved to Manchester some years later. "Ginga" from Old Brentwoods' RFC had instructed him to give me a call on arrival up north. I took the young lad out to Tiger Tiger nightclub and showed him the ropes. We started hanging out on regular occasions drinking at various student bars and we became good friends. We have remained friends ever since and laugh about the antics that used to take place when we both lived in Manchester.

Figure 8 Old Brentwoods' RFC circa 2002

But that September 2001, I spent time painting the outside of Dad's house in Epping. It hadn't been done in years and was fairly ropy. It needed quite some attention. Having been back a few weeks, Erin and I had been speaking via calling cards and emails. A romance had blossomed from our night together and I could not stop thinking about her. She was very beautiful and kind to me. Erin decided she wanted to come over to see me and I agreed gratefully. She booked her flight and we were both very excited. One day I was outside painting and my sister called. She told me to turn on the TV and that Erin would not be coming to visit. I watched BBC in horror as I saw the World Trade Centre on fire. I watched in amazement how it bellowed smoke. I had been there three weeks prior at the bottom where the subway went to Newark airport. There was instantly a worldwide terrorist search and airport security tightened with international and domestic flights in the UK and the US halting.

I went back up to Manchester to finish my HND modules. I was allowed to apply for two-thirds of the student loan but as I had been late previously I had to pay my fees up front. Erin came over and we had a great time and I finished off my modules within a few months. The University wouldn't let me graduate until the following July 2002. I played rugby for the University but only played second team. Ben Cromey was still captain and said that he needed a regular player to be based in the 1st team and seeing as I would be leaving it wasn't how he wanted to choose his team. That's what he told me anyway. I never knew if it was fact or fiction but I had fun all the same. I met Gwyn Evans the 2nd team captain. He looked like he could handle himself and I had prank called him saying I was going to sort him out one day for a fight he had had with Stu Hook. He asked me if I was Trigger in the student bar and I told him no because I thought he was going to sort me out. He was a horrible little Welsh man who was fun to say the least. I remember sleeping in his bed one night after a night out. He was at his girlfriends and I woke up all itchy convinced he had bed bugs. You never wanted to receive a pint from Gwyn. He would pluck pubic hairs from himself and put them in your pint without you knowing as a joke. One night in the Pav student bar on campus, I was in for one of his horrible surprises. He tried to give me a pint of beer mixed with urine. Wanker! He nearly got me. Gwyn's face light up with laughter as he saw how disgusted I was. Dave Coulter lived with Gwyn. He was from Bournemouth had a shaved head and I thought he was American as he was wearing an Abercrombie t-shirt and at the time this brand had hardly hit the UK shops. He was actually half Italian and we would have a laugh. He also played on the wing. The lads had been kicked out of Wellington Street West and were now living somewhere else. Apparently the landlord had come round to see such a horrific sight in the flat that he kicked everyone out. I won't go into details but it was pretty grim. I went back to live at Rosehill court for a few months and Erin came over as planned to visit me from the USA. It was great the rugby guys loved her and she came to watch me play at freshers' trail. I played a bunch of games and continued to work back at Loaf nightclub earning a bit of money. I would look after the delivery each Tuesday hung over as hell after a Monday night session with the rugby lads. On one rugby occasion we all went to "Mutz Nutz" where I was arrested for fighting. I lost my necklace Abel had given me in Daytona and was put in the back of a police van. I was taken to Bootle Street police station and put in a cell all night. At 5 am I was let go. I do remember parts of the fight but lets just say I wont go into detail. Some of the other rugby lads had provoked it and I guess it had gone too far and that I gave into peer pressure to take the law into my hands. As we were all wearing University ties and blazers every single one of us was kicked out of the nightclub and once out on the street tempers flared again. This is when I felt officer plod grab me and the handcuffs were on.

I stayed around Manchester for a few months and then decided to go and see Erin in the USA. We were in love and I pined for her massively keeping me awake at night, missing her. I went over for three weeks of Thanksgiving and had an amazing time with her and her lovely family. We partied in Cleveland and then in Pittsburgh. I remember having a lot of fun.

So once back in England I waited until January 2002. I had finished my modules and I was waiting to graduate but I was still owed a student loan instalment of about £1,000. Erin and I spoke a lot. We decided maybe I should move over to be together. It was her last year at University. I mentioned that if I went back to Daytona I could earn a lot of money on Bike week and during NASCAR race week and then after a month or two move up to Ohio.

Chapter 11

So again I flew out to Orlando from London and Abel picked me up at the end of January 2002. Back then there was no Facebook or text so one email or call and my ride was secured. I stayed with Ben who had still been living there at his new place for a while. He went back to England for two weeks so I had his roof top studio a few blocks away from A1A, all to myself. It was close to some of the hotels and the beach so a very good location. I could still walk to Palermo's, the Italian restaurant Ben and I had worked in the previous year. It was being taken over by two new people. John and Agi were having marriage problems. They were selling up and it looked like they were going through a divorce too.

Ben was still working there and some days it would be very boring if there were no customers. Abel was now working at the restaurant too. He was still playing rugby. He started taking my tips that customers had left but he dismissed my suspicion of stealing and said he was just cleaning my table. He was an odd character and hanging around at his house and seeing his family confirmed things were not quite right with his big brothers. I suspected they were involved with illegal activities but I was young and naïve and I couldn't be sure.

I played a few games for Daytona as the 15's spring season had started. I remember playing against Tampa at home and being smashed by big guys. I remember chipping a tooth somehow. I also remember another time an English team St. Neots from Bedfordshire were touring with Orlando. I couldn't wait to play against my English counterparts. I'm sure they thought the American team would be a walk over. We stuffed them. Not sure the heat helped in our favour but we won convincingly. I played both games that day and remember dump tackling their wing and getting a few cheers from the sideline. I also made a nice kick at full time from the touchline that sailed over despite having cramp in my calf muscles from playing so much.

Erin flew down to visit me on her spring break. She had a few days with me and by this stage I had moved next door to the restaurant, to hotel efficiency. Effectively it was a room with a small kitchen and bathroom. I would pay about $130 per week.

We went up to Jacksonville to play them. It was only about an hour north of Daytona on the highway. I remember it had been very wet and the ground was very soft. I was playing fly half. I remember being sin binned for allegedly spear tackling someone. Apparently in John Seldon's eyes, who happened to be the ref, (who incidentally wanted to be everyone's friend in the bar but was a complete fool on the field) it was dangerous and deserved 10 minutes for my troubles. I would watch from behind the posts. I was slightly embarrassed as Erin had come to watch me play. Doc was dating another one of his funny girls who had flown down from Illinois. He had met her on spring break. Erin had the privilege to sit next to her screaming and yelling for Doc and the team. I switched sides on one break and went blind. The flanker just tracked me across and smashed me forcing me to slide for what seemed eternity. It was a good tackle leaving me a little sore and jaded to say the least. We lost the game and always seemed to be on the back foot. I was a little embarrassed in front of Erin. It was her first rugby game and I wanted to impress her. We had a few beers and set off back to Daytona.

In March, I was in communication with Jerry in New York. John the owner from the restaurant bought me a Verizon wireless mobile phone that I paid for when the bill came. Jerry said the team were going to Savannah Georgia for a St. Patrick's Day tour. There would be a tournament. Lance the new captain was excited to have me play. We had not met but they said if I wanted to come up and bring some players it would be good fun. I asked Doc and Abi if they wanted to go. Tim had come over from London. He had asked his friends to check him into the class register at University and asked one of his friends to do an exam for him. I had told him about Daytona and spring break the year before and Tim decided that he wanted a part and flew over to stay for three weeks.

So, Doc, Abi, Tim and I all set off to Savannah about three hours north of Daytona. We all squeezed into Doc's sweaty, smelly VW golf. We met up with the Long Island rugby lads and checked into a hotel. They had booked plenty of rooms with big double beds very close to the end of the main street where all the bars were.

I met Jerry and the other lads including English Steve and a funny big guy called Raver who I would be shacking up with. Tim would share with Major Matt another scrum half who got his name from being in the military obviously. I met "Lance", "Baby Lou", "The Freak", "Birdie" and the rest of the rugby lads. I introduced Doc and Abi, too, and the beers started flowing. The next day of the tournament we were doing quite well. I played a bunch of positions and we were all enjoying the day. Jerry split his head open and there was plenty of claret pouring out. One game I was kicking the points. I missed two relatively easy kicks and a woman started heckling from the side. I stepped up again for a penalty and managed to slot it over. Finally I silenced the foul-mouthed dragon on the side. We ended up wining the tournament. That night we went out and got pretty drunk drinking green beer due to it being St Patrick's day and having girls flash us in exchange for beads. We would bar hop down the main street next to the river. The lads took care of us especially me and bought a few extra rounds. I took about $400-500 that I had earned from working hard during bike week and NASCAR week in the restaurant. Steve got arrested. A cop was on horseback just as we came out of the hotel. I put my beer can down and walked away. Steve also had one and got busted. Poor guy the cop arrested him and took him to jail for the night. He would have to pay a big fine for having an open container of alcohol. He tried to snitch me up too to the police officer, what an idiot.

One other lad, Keith, who would have made a line backer at a University in Long Island would get lucky with one local lady who was also partying and having fun at the St. Patrick's Day festival. About 20 of us took it in turns to watch through the window of him in action laughing cheering and heckling at him.

That night I had perhaps a little too much to drink. Partying with Tim and Abi was so much fun, drinking beers, shots and anything we could get our hands on. Extremely intoxicated after stumbling home and pounding a few more beers in the room, I would have a little accident in the bed. I woke up in a wet patch not very happy. Matt had gone running so I crawled into bed with Tim on to a nice dry bed. When Matt got back he thought it rather weird what I had done; considering I was a friend with Tim from the UK he thought it even weirder. He climbed into the bed I had been in and realised what had happened. He would lay briefly on the wet patch in bed with big Raver the other rugby guy sharing in the room. The next day I would get a lot of stick for that one. Not very good form I have to say. We drove back to Daytona and I said goodbye to the Long Island lads. It had been a great result and a great trip.

Chapter 12

That Easter I moved up to Cleveland because of Erin. It was the next step I needed to take. I made some arrangements for jobs, called a rugby team again and found myself a place to stay near Erin's. I took a greyhound up and it took 29 hours. The night before I left I stayed at Ben's. I went out with Abi and got very drunk. The idea was to get so drunk and tired that I'd just pass out on the bus and wake up at my destination. I got to the bus terminal around 6 am. I then woke up about 4-5 pm later in southern Georgia. The bus was about one third of the way. It was nowhere near what I had expected to be. There were hours of driving ahead of us in a cramped seat. I can tell you hung over, it was not very comfortable.

In Cleveland, I joined the Eastern Suburbs RFC. Erin would take me to practice or John Hummel the short ball coach would pick me up. I landed a job at an Italian restaurant called Geraci's near Erin's house and weekends I worked in a bar downtown called The Blind Pig collecting bottles, throwing out the rubbish.

We had an OK team and some of the John Carrol University boys played. We had one good French winger called Fred. He didn't speak much English but was a nice guy and good player. The captain, Teddy, was an arsehole to everyone. We played games against Detroit, the other team from Cleveland, Dayton and various others. I would start cancelling work to party on Saturdays, something that didn't go down well and I was fired for cancelling one time and then coming in to drink in the nightclub. The rugby wasn't great but I'm glad I did it. I did miss the Daytona boys, as I had no real friends in Cleveland or any one else to hang out with apart from Erin.

That summer Erin and her family went down to Florida. They had a timeshare condo there and it was here a previous year in 2001 that I had met Erin while she was in town. We drove down in two cars with her Mum and Dad, little sister and grandmother.

It was their annual holiday. I was excited to see Doc and the other boys. One day after my birthday I went to training. Dave, Erin's dad, and his mate came along to watch. They had heard of rugby but never seen it. I perhaps was fuelled by their attendance and wanted to impress my spectators who had made the trip especially. Towards the end of the session I miss tackled Carlos. I stopped, as I needed to catch my breath. It was a few minutes later and my heart was still beating pretty quickly. Doc came over and the session seemed to stop. Basically, it was an excuse for the tired bodies running around in the humid and hot Florida evening to also stop. Doc thought I might have had a collapsed lung. I got slightly worried. We thought it best we head to the hospital where the year previously I had got my stitches. I again had no medical insurance. In the car my hands started to curl inwards and my jaw started to lock. I became very light headed and started to panic a bit. Dave's friend then spoke and said "Quick lets get him to the hospital I think he's having a heart attack" I arrived and my heart was at 208 beats per minute even though I hadn't been running for about 15-20 minutes. I was scared as hell and didn't know what the hell was happening. I prayed not to die. I was scared, really scared. They gave me some kind of injection maybe the opposite to adrenaline. They took some blood samples and all was clear. It was horrible. They described me as having PSVT Paroxysmal Supraventricular Tachycardia, a heart condition with symptoms of palpitations, chest pressure, and light-headedness. I was pretty worried. They said it was quite common in guys my age. The copious vodka red bulls I had the night before at my birthday, stress over running or just a coincidence could have brought it on. They did suggest that the drug in my asthma spray could trigger these issues and speed up the heart. All the same, none of my friends had it and I didn't like the fact that this had happened to me. I was told when I get back to England to have it checked out. I returned that summer and sure enough did have various checks including electrocardiograms and ultrasounds. Nothing really came up but they just told me there was a conduction problem and my heart was sending too many electrical impulses for the heart to beat or pump the blood around my body. They said this could be rectified with an operation involving a catheter up my groin to the area of the heart. I did not like the idea of that and went away thinking they were talking absolute nonsense. It wasn't life threatening so I didn't think an operation was necessary for something that may have been a one off.

Chapter 13

That summer I worked at Sports Café in London and saved up money for my University year ahead. I had now graduated my Higher National Diploma from Salford University. My Dad came up for my graduation with Ann at the Lowary Centre in Salford quays.

So September 2002 I went back up to Manchester. Dad and Ann drove me up and we met up with some of the rugby lads for a drink at the Hyde Park Corner Pub or HPC, as Johnny Sadler would call it. They had wine on tap...a classy place. Cromey and Johnny Sadler were living together at Trinity Riverside. Dave Coulter aka DC for short was the lad I had met the year before. He was a winger who was mates with Gwyn Evans. He and I would live in the same house on campus at Castle Irwell. It was on the dark side. Dan Tucker who looked like Prince William also lived nearby. Dan was a good-looking bastard, would live a few doors down from DC and myself. That week we had freshers' trials. One night that I was at training I started having that scary crazy heart palpitation again. I was pretty worried. I told the coach I had to go, it was an emergency. I grabbed my stuff from the Castle Irwell training field and legged it past the houses on campus and called for an ambulance. I knew I really had about 20-30 minutes to get sorted or I would collapse. Back then I had no idea how to control it and would panic very easily which would probably make it worse. I was taken to hospital and stayed there over night having various electro-cardiograms and ultrasounds. Some of the lads came down that night to see how I was, as they were worried. Dave Coulter, James Breakhall aka "Campus Joke" and Gwyn. Gwyn would pull at all the cables attached to my heart beat monitor and joke about. It was quite funny. Helen Roche a nice young northern girl who I knew came down as well. She seemed pretty worried. She had been out that night and someone had told her about me so she would come to see me at Hope Hospital. I was discharged the next day they just kept me in over night for observation.

I was now studying BSc Media Technology at Salford University. Because I had done the HND, I would go straight into the second year. The course was pretty tough and I would have lots of questions to ask my lecturers. I would take the Wednesdays off to play. We had some great players and I became good friends with one guy especially. His name was Tim Medwell. He was lanky as hell. Big nosed, funny, dry sense of humour a lesser good-looking version of me perhaps. His stride was second to none. Calling himself "Crazy Legs" he would also pick up the nickname "Medders". He was always picked at fullback for 1st team. What I liked about him was his ability to hit great lines at pace. He also had a lethal boot on him and could kick for miles. Apparently when he was younger his father, who I later went on to meet, called Don, said to Tim, "I don't want Webb I want Blanco" referring to the great French fullback Serge Blanco instead of boring Jonathon Webb. Medders was playing at Didsbury Toc H, funnily enough in Didsbury. By the end of that year we would become good mates and went out together most Monday nights. He was my drinking buddy on the Wednesday rugby socials. The only problem was that Medders wasn't a great drinker and always refused to do a dip and down or a mucky pint. Some how he would always get away with it.

That Autumn I would get tickets for England v New Zealand and England v South Africa through Bernie our coach and his team of Trafford MV. I came down to London excited. I'd seen the All Blacks at school around 1992 when I was at Campion but I never really appreciated just what I was witnessing. I bought Erin the ref link so she could hear what was being said by the ref. It was a fantastic game at a packed out Twickenham stadium. I got to see the famous Jonah Lomu play and score. I always wanted to be a no.14 winger knowing that if I ever

100

became a good player I would get to mark Lomu my opposite no.11 wing. Jonah Lomu scored twice that day. One should have been disallowed as later I reviewed the slow motion replay that Mike Tindall's leg had held the ball up. I saw Jonny Wilkinson single handily win the game kicking point after point and scoring a great individual try through a chip and chase under the sticks.

The tickets weren't cheap but I really wanted to go and bought them by using my overdraft. I wanted Erin to watch a game of Rugby. I knew she would love the day out the atmosphere and I wanted her to see some English culture, a day at the rugby. I sold the two South African tickets for double their value and was pretty chuffed as this then paid for my All Black tickets. However police later picked these up when they had arrested the ticket tout. Apparently there are laws about exchanging tickets for larger sums of money than face value. Trafford MV's name was on the ticket and they were banned for a year. I felt pretty bad about it but I had no idea of the laws etc I was just trying to make some money seeing what I thought of as a business opportunity. I was offered a couple of hundred for my All Black tickets but declined the offer. I'm glad I did.

One time I was out with Ben in Manchester. I was hung over from the night before and it was mid afternoon. I had a heart palpitation and Ben had to drive me to Manchester Royal Infirmary as my heartbeat raced up to 200 beats per minute. I stayed in all night, which meant I missed the Salford University team photo. I was gutted. Ben Cromey joked and said "Don't worry we will have a cardboard cut out of you mate."

The start of the spring we had exams and then the rugby BUSA league finished. BUSA stands for British Universities Students Association and is the governing body for University sports in the UK. We would play Keele in the final. If we won that we were promoted. We boasted a strong side and I went on to score two tries in that game. I came off with 10 minutes to go and

Bernie called me over "Well played Liam...and I'd like a word" referring to the problem of the sold tickets and his club being banned from International ticket allocation from the RFU. Ben Cromey was taking a conversion and later said he was put off as he could hear me explaining some pathetic excuse in my cockney accent. We went on to have a great picture of the team spraying champagne that made the Student Direct newspaper.

Chapter 14

So in the summer of 2003, I decided I was going to go and play rugby back in Florida. I had split up from Erin now and wanted to do my own thing, to travel, have fun and play rugby. Tim had given me a great send off down Deansgate locks and we had a lot of fun. I arranged with BUNAC (British University North America Committee) an agency that administered foreign student exchange from Britain to the USA. They gave me a three-month student-working visa. It was a J1 status, the same as I had, had for working on the summer camp a few years before. I would be working at Alexi Bairstow's hotel and timeshare. I flew into the usual Orlando airport. Alexi was the fly half of the team. Tim my friend from Essex also arranged to have a J1 so we could both work over in the USA for the summer. The deal was that we would work during the day, party at night. The first night I arrived I was completely shattered and lost everyone instantly on the night out. Alexi had lent me $40. I hadn't been to the bank. I had left my suitcase at his house in Ormond Beach but I had no idea of his address. I managed to get a cab halfway up and completely drunk was rapping with some local guys but I had no money for the taxi. I continued to walk up north of A1A the main duel carriageway towards where he lived maybe three miles past the Spiniker Hotel resort that he was the manager of. I started getting rather worried completely intoxicated and now I was in an area with no streetlights. I flagged down a police car. I explained what had happened that I was English, jet lagged, extremely drunk and needed him to help me. He asked where I would be working and drove me back to the hotel. He asked the receptionist to call Alexi. She tried several times and I had no idea of his home address. The cop told her I must stay there in the lobby or a room somewhere for my safety. I stayed there overnight and woke up wondering how the hell I got there and in that state. Doc came to pick me up and drove me to Alexi's place. We were going on a road trip up to North Carolina. It was the Cape Fear 4th July weekend rugby 7s tournament. Doc said it was apparently quite a big popular nationwide tournament. There were a few of us that went up. Travelling up in the van was Dave Yeager, Doc, Meat, Gary Wolyzn, John Seldon and myself. We drove up through Georgia, South Carolina and then into North Carolina. There was one guy Jared Rose who was pretty quick. He went to Stetson University about 40 minutes from Daytona. We had played a practice game against them which was pretty good fun and this is where I had met Jared. We had to drive via Alexi's place to pick up my clothes for the weekend. He was fast asleep and just woke up. He had no idea what had happened in the hotel the night before. We hit the road and started our nine-hour drive north. I would explain to everyone what had happened with my little escapade the night before into the early hours. I would fall asleep and then wake up. Apparently, I would repeat my story again and again each time slightly differently to the previous. Everyone found it highly amusing that's for sure. A few hours from our destination bearing in mind we had a mini van I'm not sure where from, one of our tyres blew. It was pretty alarming. John luckily gained control and we pulled over to the hard shoulder. We either called the breakdown service or we changed the tire ourselves but I can't remember. It could have been worse than it was considering it was on the highway and we were going at least 70 miles an hour. We were back on the road and very much looking forward to getting to our destination in North Carolina.

We arrived that evening and I had just about sobered up and recovered. We all went out for a few drinks and at the end of the night everyone went back to the hotel except Jared, Doc and myself. We were enjoying the ladies' local southern accents and found ourselves at one bar at the back. We were sat at a table and Jared would imitate my accent thinking it was great way to get the attention of girls. However, one guy at a table near us jumped up abruptly and shouted "Do you guys have a problem with me and keep laughing" We were all pretty shocked. The guy was huge and I'm sure could have taken out all three of us. I told him no one had an issue and that even though I was English I was here celebrating his and my friend's national holiday of 4th July. Once he realised I was British he started to apologise. He said "Ohh man I just came back from Iraq I'm sorry, I'm pretty messed up right now. I trained with a load of British guys, you guys kick arse man". Suddenly the situation was diffused and he wanted to be my bum chum. It was hardly surprising from someone so fickle.

The next day we played against some tough teams. It was brutally hot and quite dry compared to that of Florida where it is usually so humid. I remember there was a bald English ref. It was so hot and he became so dehydrated that he had to have an intravenous drip to rehydrate him. There were certainly some nice looking female spectators. I played at fly half, Doc was mainly at scrum half and Dave Yeager at centre. I would perform my usual dummy, scissors pop…and against the less talented sides it worked. We picked up a couple of military guys on the way who helped prop our team up.

We played against one team Life, a Chiropractor University from Atlanta, Georgia. They were pretty good and well structured and put a few points on the board. It was my first experience of playing a team far superior and I couldn't wait to get off the field. We didn't do too well but Jim Smorto also filmed the games, which was nice.

Then later that summer we went down to Port St. Lucie and a place called Stuart, which was half way down to West Palm Beach from Daytona. I was playing well and scored quite a few tries. Tim still hadn't arrived yet he was waiting for his visa to be processed in the post from the US embassy in London. I took the eye of a young lady called Stacey. She would give me the title "London Boy". Unfortunately, "Meat" one of the players was quite a brutal player but rather clumsy. I hurt my leg when we collided. I couldn't play any more and went to get an x-ray. I was given a pain killer shot in my arse and I was discharged. It wasn't broken or fractured but I left with crutches. The rest of the summer I was rather miserable and had to take two weeks off work because of my leg. I had no money and Tim had to help me out which obviously he wasn't too happy about. I was living with Tim now as he had finally moved over and we were renting a hotel apartment on the beach for $600 a month between the two of us. It had two beds, a bathroom and a small kitchen. I would be in a lot of pain hobbling about especially when we walked to work with my leg all wrapped up in a bandage. I swear something was missed in the x-ray, as the pain wouldn't settle for weeks. It didn't make things easier when I had to shift heavy furniture around at the hotel sweating in the baking Florida heat and putting pressure on my bad leg. I couldn't run at practice and Lane, a loud mouth player, would just love to tease me that he was so much faster than me.

My leg eventually got better and we travelled up to Tallahassee the capital town of Florida in the north. It was home to the University known as Florida State. Apparently FHM magazine had conducted a survey that said the grocery shop called Publix was the number one pick up spot in the country. We travelled up in convoy this time it took about four hours cooped up in Doc's small car. Alexi managed to get the weekend off and his friend Kieran was over from South Africa visiting and also working in the hotel. Kieran wasn't a fan of me to be honest and I wasn't of him. Matt Meyer had sent me a case of energy drinks to Gary's address of a new brand of athletic energy-boosting liquid. I would take this along. He knew I was playing rugby and I thought that was a nice little touch. It's funny how you remember the kind little things like that people do for you.

We made it to the final. Alexi was injured; I floated out a pass with a dummy scissors. I had wound up my long pass to the wing and the opposite guy had telegraphed it well. He intercepted the ball and ran it in under the posts. It was a heart-breaking experience to have lost the game and the tournament single handily. However we partied hard as usual. Tim and myself leading the way from the front, singing renditions of "Tampax Factory", "Yogi Bear" and "I used to work in Chicago's". The bars were great fun and we all had a lot of fun. A friend of mine, Emily Burr, who was from Pensacola Florida came to watch and party with us. Emily was a well-mannered girl and lived about a few hours drive away. I had met her in the previous summer whilst she was living and studying in London as an exchange student. It was nice that she had stayed in touch and we got to see each other.

The next day, still completely hung over, we went to say hi to the lovely sorority girls we had met the night before. I had brought my Superman outfit over with me that I had purchased for the student union party called "Rec Night" at Salford University. Each team would go as a certain action hero or cartoon character. I knocked on the door asking for "Boobs Junior" and "Boobs Senior". These were two of the girls Tim and I had met the night before. There was a group of them. Others girls had named themselves printed on their tight white tank tops as "Big Boobs" and ""Baby Boobs" but each of them had a nickname that ended in "boobs". The sorority mother wouldn't answer the door. I told her I was a stripper and that the girls had paid for me so I wanted them to get their money's worth. What I didn't know was she was now calling the student campus police, who happened to be armed with .45 revolvers. I walked off empty handed while Doc and Tim were heckling from the car and filming me on Doc's old S-VHS camera. The police actually showed up. Still dressed in the Superman outfit I had bought from the Warner Brothers shop in the UK, they asked me for my ID. I told them that unfortunately I had left it on Krypton, the home of Superman. Doc told me to pipe down, as this was now quite serious. I got out the car and searched for it in the boot. The policeman seemed angry and asked why I lied about not having my passport. Obviously he hadn't heard my extremely witty joke. They soon came round. Apparently there had been a homeless guy from a few years ago who would dress up as Superman. However even though they realised it wasn't me they had to issue me with a trespass warrant. This to me was a great souvenir to take back to the UK. We said thanks to the policemen and goodbye then we set off onto the road back to Florida all rather entertained. Even though we never saw these girls again, I was content that I hadn't been arrested.

That was I think the last rugby tournament of the summer and shortly after because I had become so lazy at work Alexi had no other option than to let me go. I was mortified. The jobs he gave me in the hotel of cleaning pigeon shit from the windows, moving furniture in the blasting Florida mid day heat and cleaning windows was not my idea of the "Condo Inspector/Front Desk" he had originally promised me. I managed to get the cash, I think from my sister, to fly home although it was a complete nightmare trying to explain to people what had happened and asking them to bail me out. Now that I had no job associated with my J1 visa status I was inclined under the immigration laws to leave the country immediately.

Chapter 15

I came back to the UK to find that I had failed my second year of the degree. It was a lot harder than the HND and I hadn't really put the effort in considering I knew little about the course or the TV industry. I always struggled with University and I hadn't realised that classes alone were not enough to pass this course. This meant that I would have to repeat the year. However it was just three to four classes so this meant I could play rugby and work more in a job so I was financially more stable.

DC, Tucker and myself moved into Waterside Student Village in Salford. The houses were built about 5 years prior. It was a housing estate, more houses, with some flats but mostly three bedroom houses, like the one we had. The road names were named after the star signs in the Zodiac and the solar system, Gemini, Aquarius and Pluto etc. We had arranged everything regarding contracts, deposit etc that summer. I was repeating my second year but the other lads were in their final year. Dan was 19 and Dave was 22 a year below me. Dave studied Aeronautical Engineering and Dan was doing Geography. Dan had been 2nd team captain the previous year and now was rugby club chairman. Ben Barlow would take over from Ben Cromey as 1st team Captain as the team had been promoted to the league above. It would prove to be a difficult league with the likes of Liverpool John Moores and Manchester University playing against us.

We had the freshers' trials and I scored a brace of tries looking pretty fit from playing 7s all summer in Florida. However, I disgraced myself by attempting to head butt one of the opposition. A crazy mad moment I regret which resulted in a red card. I am sure I was also later fined with a mucky pint of some kind as well.

I was in shape and playing right wing No.14. Chris Stewart the black lad who claimed to have played at Leeds Rhinos academy was the other winger, number 11. This meant Tim Medwell would command the full back position. It would be hard to entice Ben Coulbeck to play. He was trying to make a go of things at Macclesfield RFC a semi pro Northern club. Gareth Troughton would play scrum half, Ben Cromey at fly half; Sam Harland would play inside centre and usually Ben Coulbeck at outside centre. Chris Stewart was solid and very quick except his hands were a bit hit and miss. He would sometimes give bad erratic passes but he was a good finisher.

Game days for University were on a Wednesday. If you had classes on a Wednesday you would have to skip them. I didn't want to fall into the trap like last year of skipping too many classes and failing again. We would as ever wear our suits to the game and University club tie. Tucker as club chairman would have a spare tie here and there which would always prove handy. There would be a bus laid on from University house next to the gym that would drive us to our away games. Players would bring on sandwiches and pasta for carbohydrates, bananas, Jaffa cakes and sometimes videos for us to watch or CDs with house techno music to pump us up on the journey. That autumn was to be that of the 2003 World Cup in Australia. England had had a good summer and won memorable games in the June against Australia and New Zealand. I had been able to watch these in the USA. The World Cup games would be on at 8 am in the morning London time due to the time difference. We would get up early to watch the matches. Some times we would go round to Cromey and Sadler's flat at Trinity Riverside with cans of larger. We would draw names out of the hat. If the commentator mentioned the player's name you had chosen this would inflict a fine of drinking a swig of your beer. England made the quarterfinals and DC and I went down to Waxy O' Connor's bar in the Printworks. It was against Wales. We ate our English breakfasts and watched nervously. England were losing at half time. DC arrogantly said, "Lads don't be so stupid…It's just Wales for goodness sake. We're not going to lose to them". He gave a cocky laugh but sure enough if you check the history books he predicted correctly and England bounced back winning the game well.

The following week England went on to beat France in the semi finals. I had got back with Erin after my summer away in September but Tim invited me to go away to France for a long weekend. Apparently he was to be a ski instructor the following spring and it was an orientation weekend for people to see what the company does and what was expected of them. Tim told me that as it was his friend that ran the company I should come along. I made up a terrible excuse for work at the restaurant and went to Macclesfield where the bus was leaving. The bus would travel down to London then the South Coast to catch the ferry over to France and plough on over night to the French Alps. While Tim and I were in the resort of Val d'Isère the Rugby World Cup Final between England and Australia took place the other side of the world. We woke up at 8 am with it being evening in Australia. We went to a local bar completely hung over but had another beer to ease the pain and to get into rugby drinking mode. Wilkinson and Flately exchanged penalties and after Lote Tuqiri's sixth minute try, Jason Robinson went over to score a great worked team try in the corner. We celebrated in a similar fashion to Jason Robinson although there were no balls to fist into the air. We were still in this game Tim and I thought. The game finished even and there was to be extra time. I went outside the bar for some fresh air and came back in to find Australia had kicked a penalty. It was neck and neck all the way but they were now in front. Tension was high and some Australian and English supporters in the French bar we were in almost clashed. Someone had an inflatable kangaroo as a mascot for the day and one lad popped it with his cigarette out of disgust. There were a few minutes to go. Then the famous kick came from Jonny Wilkinson. It sailed over and the bar erupted. Minutes later the final whistle was blown. Everyone jumped up and went mental. I managed to bang my head on one of the ceiling wooden beams and nearly knocked myself out as I jumped on Tim and celebrated. It was a special moment to witness such a national memory with Tim a mile up in the French mountains.

One game for University we travelled up to York. I felt good. The conditions were good and I was looking forward to playing. More so to repeat the partying that took place in 1999 when I had played against the second team and stayed with my cousin who happened to be studying there. I had already set up one try and had one disallowed. I felt like it was only a few minutes until I scored. I kept knocking on the York University door. It was probably the most confident I had been, all season. I was running off my right wing to the left of the field linking up and looking for lots of work. I stayed extremely interested and wanted nothing more than the ball and to score. I just knew I was playing well and very confident with the sort of teammates around me. It's hard to describe but that's how I felt. Not long into the game I felt a pain in my groin. Not a muscle pain but a throb. At first I thought my boxers were caught in my testicles somehow. After running on a bit, I adjusted again and looked down to see my now rather large testicles. I freaked out somewhat, as you do I guess. I called Medders over who was a student nurse at the time. He was running late but had raced over to York in his old school battered up blue Ford Fiesta who he had named "Dwayne". He said "Get to Hospital straight away". I didn't want to be subbed, as it didn't seem bad. Apparently the quote I gave was "Ref... Ref I have massive balls!" I was hoping it could be treated as a blood bin but the game went on regardless without me. I was taken to the local Accident and Emergency where a couple of doctors poked at me and prodded me. They said it was a burst blood vessel. How on earth I had done that I was thinking? They had swollen quite a lot by now. Maybe it was from the deep heat that had got onto my skin. Maybe it was from the tight cycling shorts I had worn to keep everything together so to speak and it had compressed everything a little too much. Who knows? All I remember was that my two testicles were now one and I wanted it fixed as soon as possible. After an ultrasound (as the doctors wanted to rule out a hernia) they informed me that there was nothing they could do. If they drained the blood it may get infected. So they said I must leave it and wait. They had already started turning purple and weighed a ton. It was a rather weird feeling that I do not wish to have again. I didn't take too well to having balls that felt they might drop off at any point due to the increased new weight on them. I think Tim came to pick me up from the hospital and drove a miserable Liam back to Manchester. We met up in the student bar and at that time when Waxy O' Connor's pub in the Printworks was sponsoring us I distinctively remember Duffy pretending to punch me in the balls as he found this rather funny seeing me flinch. I could have killed him for that. Needless to say I was pretty sore for the next week. It became my new party trick to show what had happened. One player said if I had had an extra penis due to the size of the swelling I could have played space hopper and bounced around on it. I missed the game next week. I hated missing games. I hated being a sub. I think I preferred to play a full game for the second team. Once, Ben Barlow said he was playing me the 1st half and then he would take me off at half time regardless. Not what most captains would have done but that was his pre-meditated decision that was out of my control. I knew I had to do something and this inspired me more as a player to get involved. One phase deep in their 22 meter I found myself as first receiver. Not usually able to create something, I darted over the line and went over to score what seemed an easy try. This game that I missed happened to be against Hull University. I had played them a few years back with the likes of Sadler and Cromey up at their place. I decided to stay involved and to borrow one of the broadcast DVCPro50 cameras from the University. I had no idea how to use it but I went down to document what went on to be an epic win for Salford University. There were two great tries from Tim Medwell and fantastic runs from Chris Stewart. I was commentating too from the sideline and we had lots of 2nd team players and friends who came down to support us in the Manchester drizzle. It turned out to be our only victory in the League of the year 2003-4. I obviously didn't play, that might tell you something but I edited the footage on the University software adding a build up to the game, a voiceover, some music and some basic graphics. I was so into the production that during the game I went onto the pitch to film from behind Ben Cromey taking a penalty. The referee was furious "Can you get that camera off the pitch please"…"Yes boss whatever you want boss" was my cheeky reply. It was a tough year for captain Ben Barlow. We had a great team but somehow we were just out of our depth against more organised stronger teams. I remember one game Ben was forced to either kick us out of trouble or would kick long for territory. I chased everything down, tired on the wing I refused to chase down the final kick. This didn't go down very well. But the game was lost and I was tired. Tim Fourrie, the number 8 from local club Sedgley Park RFC, had come down for a training session to explain and teach to us the importance of the breakdown defensively with guards and bodyguards crucial to be implemented during a game.

One of our last games at home was against Liverpool University. We were sitting near the bottom of the table with just that one win over Hull. It had been a long season and everyone was slightly frustrated and to be honest, bored with losing. We were again out played by the Merseyside team and found ourselves camped on our own try line maybe 10 meters out. We had a scrum. Ben could have kicked but we were going up hill. I popped up outside Ben Cromey who was playing in his usual fly-half position. To my surprise he popped me the ball. I don't know why I arched round the back of him and why I didn't act as a decoy on his inside that I quite commonly did but that's how I chose my run and angle. I was through the gap and now racing away. I had one defender to beat the full back and 50 meters to go. I stepped off my stronger left leg and accelerated again from him as I continued running. The line was getting closer. I was in the 22 nearing the line. I knew the camera was on me. Duffy was filming from the side with one of the cameras I had borrowed from my University media facilities department. My legs began to tire. Surely I wouldn't make it. People had come down to watch and hadn't seen any entertainment from us all game. I dived over the line and collapsed. Try time indeed. Seconds later the mad Sam Perrin, jumped on me and hugged me. Apparently this try had been the next best thing for him who had been chasing me all the way in support from the original scrum. I couldn't breath. Not only did I just run 90-meters uphill towards the end of a game of rugby but also I had a muscular flanker hugging and squeezing me to death. It was one of those tries that didn't win us the game or make a dent in the score deficit. In fact they were almost a cricket result ahead of us but my sheer belief in scoring seemed to lift the guys and they rejoiced as if we had won the damn game.

Tim Medwell and I had been great friends. We became very close friends in fact. He was like a rugby guru on the pitch and a life mentor off the field. I always liked listening to his advice. He was a positive guy with a relaxed sensible approach, although he was like me at the times, terrible with money and finishing his studies. He did seem to see things in perspective and thought rationally about them as well. Tim used to come over after training or if he couldn't make it would come to our house at Waterside student village to pick me up. I would cook up a mushroom, bacon, tomato and basil pasta dish to fill us up before a night of drinking. Dan and Dave always seemed to have assignments to do, especially Dave whose Aeronautical engineering had a lot of maths including immensely horrible algebra. Tim and I would go to Tiger Tiger nightclub on Mondays to party at their event called "Vodka Island" We knew the girl on the door, Catherine, who would always sort Tim and me free passes for the VIP room. This would open later on in the evening so we would queue jump and usually get a double vodka red bull and bottle of Stella each to mix things up. We would take to our usual table and watch all the other excited young naïve students line up in the cold weather and slowly enter the premises.

Chapter 16

That spring of 2004 we went to Spain for the University rugby tour. I hadn't been on tour with the University since 2000 and I was excited to go. Dave Coulter, who had been social secretary all year, had done a fine job organising fancy dress, taxis and the establishments where we would drink. Along with Dan Tucker, the Chairman, they would both arrange the tour shirts. My nickname on the back was Trigger and it had no.14 printed on it. My tour name was "Rocky". Somehow I gained this after walking down Seaford Road on the way to training on campus. As we walked together down the road I had suspected that some locals who looked like they were going to attack us, might indeed do so. I picked up a small rock in case of any trouble. Cromey, Coulter and Tucker were with me on their way to training too and thought I was some kind of psycho about to unleash an all out onslaught attack. Bearing in mind this street was notorious for attacks and muggings on students it seemed like a good precaution at the time. So the name stuck and this is how I gained the tour name "Rocky"

Some of the guys were going to drive down through France into Northern Spain on the bus that was part of the package the students were offered. A lot of the Freshers would go and the senior players too. Tim would look at cheap flights from Stansted to Girona outside Barcelona and he would look at hotels too online. Our flights were pretty cheap. I think we just had to pay tax as we booked them so far in advance. We went a few days earlier. In the words of Tim "To acclimatise." We flew over from Stansted. Tim drove us both down from Manchester in his battered Ford Fiesta, Dwayne. We would pass Leicester where his Granny was from and we stayed at my Dad's house. The next day, we went to visit my Italian Grandmother in Ilford. As a student nurse Tim was great with old ill people.

I managed to get my future brother-in-law's father to drive us to the airport for £20. We got stuck in traffic and were panicking but we made the flight over that was about two and half hours in duration.

Tim and I were happy to be away ahead of all the other students. We felt more grown up taking the flight rather than a 30-hour bus journey through Europe. We were in another hotel to the lads but it happened to be the same hotel as Tim Walker's who was also on tour with Surrey Roehampton University playing football. He gave himself his own tour name of "Arnold Quarterni**er" and seeing as he was quarter Jamaican this fitted well.

I remember that Tim and I would run through the streets one day, me on one side of the road and him on the other passing the ball to each other dodging locals and cars alike. The local Spanish thought we were mad and weren't really sure what sport the weird looking ball was from.

That night we went out to one of the local nightclub/discothèques. It looked as if it was a teen night as most of the clients were extremely young. Tim and I just propped up the bar and drank. We met a guy called Leo. He was from Argentina and was the manager. We explained to him that there would be hundreds of English students coming in a day or two from many different sports teams and many different English Universities. Leo was excited. His eyes lit up in $$$ or in his in his case €€€€. We suggested that maybe we could work for the club "Snoopies" and that we would make sure he would get plenty of clients. Most English like to bar hop so it was inevitable that some if not all of the rugby players and the rest of the teams would stumble into his place whether or not we helped promote it or not. We made a deal that he would give us €40 per night each and 5 free drinks. It sounded quite low but all we had to do was hand out flyers from 9 pm until 1 am. He took us for a coffee and a cigarette and we began the painstaking, boring flyering on the streets enticing girls and guys alike to the club. Most were surprisingly sober and it was hard work being fobbed off although there was some banter between potential customers and us. The rugby team arrived and couldn't believe what Tim and I were doing. They thought we were mad, to come over for a rugby tour to party and there we were ending up working for peanuts. We finished early and in between we would hand over a token of some sort to the bartender who gave us strong mixed drinks. Kendrick, who incidentally was dressed as a nun, started a fight with the Surrey Roehampton boys. Apparently the quote from Kenny was "I'm not hard...I'm fucking mental". They too were all in fancy dress and Kenny took on about four of them who all seemed to bottle it and run off. It was a funny night for Tim and me although it was probably not the best night of our lives. We told Leo the next day that to be honest we wanted to see our friends and although we had had fun, it was probably time to say thanks and do our own thing. Truth be told we wanted part of the mayhem of being on tour, getting drunk and running riot too. It certainly wasn't any fun seeing the rest of the lads do it without us. Leo agreed that it was OK not to work any more. Somewhat disappointed, he agreed he would pay us at the end of the week. I remember guessing that this was probably when everyone else got paid. So we would get paid the same time as all the other workers including, security, bar staff, cleaners etc and perhaps even Leo himself. It seemed a bit dodgy for him as he kind of fobbed us off but he did end up paying us. The next day we had learnt that Duffy had had two epileptic fits on the bus on the way down through Europe. He still carried on drinking and smoking as he normally would, otherwise it just wasn't the same Duffy.

The day of the rugby tournament we waited for the bus outside our hotel that was about ten minutes walk from the rugby guys. We boarded the bus and it took us to the field about twenty minutes away. We arrived and none of our rugby lads were there. I managed to get hold of someone, probably Ben Barlow who was captain. They said that the bus hadn't picked them up and that they had been waiting. The drivers informed me that they didn't pick up from their hotel. Apparently the pick up point was at ours. They kindly agreed to go back and get the lads and seemed somewhat concerned that it was necessary to go back and get the rest of the team. This is what we did. By the time we got to the lads' hotel, everyone had already made plans to carry on drinking to nurture their hangovers or perhaps go back to sleep. Apparently, there had been some confusion about what time or where the bus was picking everyone up. It took everything in Medders and myself to persuade them all, tough job to be honest and I'm not sure how we managed to round up the troops. We all boarded the bus and got to the field. It was a nice warm day and there was a nice cool breeze. It would heat up later though. We played a bunch of games and surprisingly everyone did pretty well. I was enjoying the day and put away a few tries. We headed into the knock out stage. We played against Hull, the University I had not had a chance to play against earlier in the year. This time though I had no such testicular issues or cringing groin injuries. I managed to break away only to be tap tackled that resulted in me crashing to the hard floor. I hadn't been held and quickly got to my feet and sprinted ahead to score. One game, I was show boating after scoring a try and was given a stern talking to by the referee that this was not something that he allowed during the matches he was in charge of. We ended up making the final and Tim proposed we have the national anthem. We went on to win. It was a big surprise to have won it, especially if you look back on the state some people were in that morning. The only silverware Ben Barlow would win that year except there wasn't a cup or trophy presented just the honour of winning. We then went on to have a court session in one of the local bars called "Sinatra's". The committee members organised this with the bar and they also organised the fines. There would be a judge, jury, defence council and prosecution. I was chief snitch as always in charge of dobbing people in for crimes committed during the court session (swearing, using mobile phone and wrong handed drinking). Each individual would be fined for some kind of heinous misdemeanour he had committed throughout the rugby year. DC was in charge with Tucker and Barlow also on the panel. Whoever was brought forward, never got off lightly. We shared the court session with the football lads. Traditionally the rugby and footy lads didn't get on but somehow players united in someway that previously hadn't happened. The rivalry had stopped and we regarded them as comrades instead of the infidel. There started to be a bit of nakedness during one fine. It was called a Hawaii 5-0. This was when everyone would throw beer on the person to initiate them. Therefore he would get completely soaked with beer from head to toe while naked, hence the name Hawaii 5-0 from the television program. I won't even go into details about what a golden boot was. Mark Fraser decided to film such a funny exhibition on his mini DV home camera. Some how the local police had been either told or had been passing by randomly. This sort of behaviour was not tolerated over there in Spain. A large group of us had congregated outside the bar cheering, singing and shouting, plus this one football lad was stark naked. The police came and started beating people with their trunchons. Mark Fraser who was filming had his camera yanked from him by one of the officers. It was on a strap around his neck. The commotion was quite alarming especially to the footy lad that was naked and being beaten by a cop. Luckily one of the hockey girls knew how to speak pretty good Spanish. She spoke with the police and negotiated to let the boys go without any arrests. The police though seemed like they were more concerned about the footage of the incident especially as a policeman had beaten someone innocently on camera. The situation was calmed down and everyone was allowed to return to drinking, fully clothed though. It was pretty exciting and entertaining but also rather intimidating and worrying. The rest of the tour was a success. On my last night I really was tired and wanted to chat up one girl who was the editor of the student direct newspaper. I think a few of the others had more chance than me so I gave up and went home to the hotel early as I was all rugby and partied out. It was a sad but intelligent way to end my tour.

Chapter 17

Later that spring I joined Manchester rugby club. I would go down on the train. I played in the second team and I was extremely proud. Manchester RFC had a great history. Back then in 2004 they were in National League 1, a league below the Premiership. Manchester RFC were based in Cheadle Hulme a nice place of Cheshire. My first game was against Bradford & Bingley. Apparently their first team had a player called Lesley Vainikolo who was playing for Bradford Bulls the Super League team. Rumour had it he was also playing for Bradford and Bingley during his off-season. Luckily for me as an 11 and a half stone winger I didn't have to come across the Tongan international 17 stone winger. I ended up scoring that day from the full back position. I used to race back to Manchester on Saturdays as I was working as a bartender. I remember how sore I'd be and then I had a nice 8-hour shift ahead of me working at Lime bar in centre of Manchester, serving pints, mixed drinks and cocktails to all the weekend partygoers. One time we went all the way up to Kendal in Cumbria. The ground was soft and playing against those farmer boys was tough. Callum Stone, a fresher for Salford, also played at scrum half. During the game, one of the players and Callum had an altercation. It resulted in Callum giving this much older prop, who incidentally looked like he'd been playing longer than Callum had been alive, a cheeky punch. It was quite funny to see this happen. It seemed to take forever to get back and I would pass out in the back of someone's car. Any sleep before work after those cold northern afternoons was a bonus. Luke Hewson our captain. He was a bald hooker who used to play at Sale RFC and apparently left around 1996 when the game turned professional. I would entice other players down like Chris Walker a well drilled prop from High Wycombe way and Zishan the number 8 for Salford University who had played at London Irish Academy with "Essex" Dave Jacobs.

The University BUSA league was over with Ben Barlow who captained on paper what would look like a good well-skilled team, but unfortunately we finished bottom of the league. Ben Cromey had captained the team before Ben Barlow and had continued to play after handing his captaincy over.

We had our AGM towards the end of term. I was one of the nominations to be the new captain. I hadn't even thought about putting myself forward even after Ramsey had mentioned it to me one day when I bumped into him on Deansgate. It was held at Waxy O Connor's pub in the Printworks in their function room where all our student nights would start out. I remember two others players were put forward, Eddie Parkes and Mark Fraser. The committee members ordered all three of us out of the function room. Mark said straight up that he wasn't bothered and didn't even want to be captain. Eddy was telling us both how much he really wanted to be captain and that he had been so all through his life at school etc he had been a leader and a captain and blah blah blah. I thought, "Turn it in mate!" I was pretty nervous. We went back into the room and sure enough Ben Cromey gave me some kind of signal that I can't remember at the time but the penny dropped later. It was agreed that apparently by unanimous decision I had been given the nod by a vote. Perhaps as I had been there so many damn years they gave it to me out of sympathy, or perhaps it was of some sort of default. But it didn't matter. Wow I thought, I have big shoes to fill. Being a captain of Salford University was a big deal. I had played under many captains. Robb Ladd, Gwyn Evans of the second team. Stu Sorrel in my early days of 1999-2001 Ben Cromey and then Ben Barlow. Now it was my turn to lead from the front. I had never been a captain before. I was never one to be a follower in life but I was never a born leader either. I usually did my own thing that turned out to be better. But on the team I would always listen and respect the captains and look up to them. Now it was my turn. I didn't really have an idea of what a captain did. I thought the best way to lead from the front was to be as fit as I could, as strong and as fast as I could, to be organised and disciplined. I trained all summer and started learning about plyometric training. It was a type of training that I wasn't used to. Adam one of the guys from the gym would show me some training exercises. He explained to me there were two types of muscles, fast twitch and slow twitch. He said for a rugby player or boxer you would mainly need the fast twitch to explode out of the blocks. He elaborated and said that the muscles needed to fire up quickly in order to make a positive motion and that plyometric training would help this. He was part of the GB team and competed in the European championships for his age and weight category. It was tough but was a great eye opener and doing this training I felt I would have an edge on the other players I would compete against, more importantly against the other captains. I realised we would not have a kicker or a fly half. Ben Cromey said he would play. Medders offered his services too. But both were working full time now. Medders was a nurse in an old people's home taking care of patients with social learning difficulties. Cromey was working in a gym as a sales manager and personal trainer.

That summer, Dad, who had a house in France, asked me if I wanted to come down and stay for a bit while I was on holiday. He had bought an old stone country house in a village in South West France a few years earlier with Ann, his long-term girlfriend. We drove down 22 hours in Dad's Lexus. Somehow my neck was in great pain perhaps from some gym or rugby work out and painkillers didn't seem to help. However, we found a local rugby team in the newspaper. Dad drove me there. The training was pretty miss match and a shambles. We arrived at the so-called pitch that was just a grassy area. There were no lines marked out and certainly no posts or flags. There was a small clubhouse and a bar. Typically French, the players were drinking pastis and smoking horrible strong French cigarettes before the training session had started. After training they told my Dad there was a tournament that weekend so I decided to play and Dad would take me. It was rather far away but Dad drove to this little club that had a small stadium with changing rooms and a stand for the spectators. It was a sevens tournament. I met the coach and a few of the players who were all about my age. I remembered how to say left and right in French, communication is always useful in rugby of course, as well as scissors or switch that they called "cross" or in French *"Croisé"* It was a nice warm day and there was a cool breeze. The club was situated at the bottom of a small valley. We played 7s rugby on half a pitch so there wasn't exactly the same room as normal. I found the French hard but at the same time rather easy to defend against. Unlike in America, where the players run round you and back their speed, the French players seemed to try and run straight through me. This turned out to be a great tackling session for me. This meant that all I had to do was get low and smash them. I was English. They could probably tell. I wanted to make a statement to these French lot and my English proud ego kicked in. Dad was watching on the sideline too. I wasn't going to let him down either I thought. He was the father of the only English lad playing. I cannot remember quite how we got on in terms of what place we finished in the tournament but it was a fun day. The big fat French coach with a moustache thanked my Dad and me for coming. I do remember the exact words he said that left me feeling proud. " *Monsieur...votre fil est très forte"* meaning," Your son is very strong" I thought I'm not strong I just wanted to smash your fellow countrymen.

Most of the summer I spent pre season training at the University gym. Adam would give me some extensive workouts that would result in me walking home and vomiting perhaps from over training. It was tough and a new level that I wasn't really used to. Some days I would take a bag of old Gilbert rugby balls down to the Castle Irwell playing fields. It was summer and the pitches had dried out quite considerably compared with what they are like during the winter months. The grass was lush and green and the wild daisies were out. It was just me and maybe the odd jogger or man walking his dog. I remember it being a very peaceful place. Although I wasn't the best kicker I did seem to get better and better. I would practise conversion kicks easy to hard and short to long distance. I would go through the 22-meter drop out situation and kick offs. I would also kick for touch. Kick after kick I practised and would usually stay for about two hours until I was satisfied. Sometimes kicking an outrageous difficult kick and other times missing them to the side. I was very inconsistent but at least I had gone down there. I would remember seeing a sign a few years previously in the gym of Erin's University. It read, *"When you aren't training, your opponent is and somewhere down the line you will have to face him".* This was the kind of inspiration that I would need to lead my team forward I thought.

That summer I trained down in Cheadle Hulme at Manchester RFC too. Every Tuesday and Thursday I would get the train and do horrible sprint sessions for pre-season. They were big lads down there and Isaac, the Kiwi personal trainer, took the session. I remember thinking that now that a few players who had left due to the relegation into National Division 2 League, this might mean there would be an opening for me in the First team. Looking back now it was rather a naive opinion but it showed I wanted to work towards something. I always felt a bit nervous around these players but keen to learn and they had some great back linc moves that I was eager to show the lads at University. I would write the plays down on paper and print them off for each player to have as a reference when the year started.

I would meet with a chap named John Livesey. He worked for the RFU. I had got to know John a year before when Cromey and I, along with DC, would work as volunteers coaching rugby and promoting the game to some of Greater Manchester's primary schools. Rugby was getting rather a lot of interest with England doing so well in the World Cup.

John was a northerner and a good bloke. He was based down at Manchester Metropolitan University building on Oxford Road. We had lunch one day in Lime bar to discuss the future of Salford University RFC. John explained that if I filled out a five year plan and designed a website using the RFU's given template, I would benefit and gain a financial bursary for the University club as a reward for my hard efforts. I met him a few times and we completed the lengthy application form. I ended up being awarded around £600-800 for the club. I'm not sure how the money was spent but it was. I was also awarded website of the month by the RFU. I received a replica gold medal that the England players won at the 2003 World Cup Final. Included in the website were photos, jokes, and videos the viewer could stream. I uploaded all these as a high and low-resolution option. Quite good for back in 2003 I thought. I even included a page for Bernie our coach with some of his favourite quotes. *"Liam, what's all this about you coming up with new moves? No one gives Jason Robinson moves, he just beats people!" "Kick them the ball give them the problem"* was another that was sure to make the page dedicated to Bernie. Bernie was old school and loved his quotes enough for us to have a chuckle at him that's for sure.

We moved out of Gemini Road on Waterside student village and I continued to work at Lime bar over the summer. I went back down south for a bit before my final year started. Tucker and DC had graduated and I moved back in on campus of Castle Irwell student village to the third year flats. While I was back down in Essex I played one game for Old Brentwoods' RFC. It was about three weeks before University started. I got there late and didn't have time to warm up. The ground was fairly hard. During the first minute I was tackled late. I felt something in my ankle go. It was painful. My heart sank. I never got injured so after some cold spray was applied I hobbled off to carry on playing. I tried to run down the wing but pulled up in pain barely able to move. I came off and iced it on the back of the van. I was now in a bit of trouble. Although Manchester rugby club did not contract me they would be annoyed, as I had injured myself playing for another team. That was not my main concern. How was I to captain my University? All those dream and hopes suddenly seemed like they would vanish and disappear. I went to the local hospital for an x-ray and waited the usual three to four hours with my Dad. I was supposed to go back up north on the train to work in the bar but I had to stay in Essex. There was no fracture and they told me it was just a very bad sprain. I wasn't given any crutches or anything. That was it; I was discharged and told to go home. I hobbled around in pain for a few days and walked around campus at a snail's pace. It eased up a bit but I couldn't train. I was so upset but slowly over a few weeks it healed. I lied to Manchester RFC and told them I fell down some stairs in a nightclub drunk. The physio did help strap up my ankle and spent a couple of sessions helping me move it by doing some short sprints with cones to help the ankle change pace at speed. I was convinced it was some kind of ligament problem. They say sometimes this can be more painful and worse than a fracture as this will heal but ligaments that are torn tend to need surgery.

Chapter 18

A few weeks later the University year started. We would have freshers' week and it would give me a chance to see what Freshers would turn up to play. One lad that seemed confident was a young lad called Stu. He had played rugby league and showed a lot of confidence. Another lad, Matt Lindsay, had also played for Leicester RFC at some colt level. Chris Tyson would be the vice captain and we met up for a meeting. He said he would make all trainings, we would select the team then I would send text messages to everyone, notifying them about game day logistics. Ben Egelneck was the Chairman and Dave Jacobs the Treasurer. Ben was a good lad. He hung out with Eddy who I'm not sure approved of me being captain, as he had wanted the job. He never said anything but I was sure of it. They lived together along with Andy Port the second team scrum half.

At freshers' trials, two lovely ladies who turned out to be physiotherapists offered their services. They were called Carla and Amy and also lived on campus. I decided that I couldn't take contact with my ankle still being somewhat injured and watched from the side line, making notes of the new players in the usual Manchester drizzle, one Sunday afternoon. Like the previous captains I had a fair idea what the other players were capable of. I was just interested in the new guys. Over time some would filter out and leave and some would get injured. That's the nature of rugby and each year's freshers' trials. We all enjoyed the freshers' pub-crawl that Porty had organised. Apparently there had not been a decision regarding who would be social secretary. It would be between Porty and Duffy. Duffy played 2nd team prop. He wasn't the best player but a top lad, loyal and always up for a beer. A local lad he could put a way a few pints that's for sure.

The big day was looming towards our first game. I was nervous and decided to play myself at fly half. Some of the other lads probably didn't like the fact I was playing there but I knew I had to be close to everyone and that I couldn't do it from wing or fullback. Plus we had players that could play in the back three and I wanted a more hands on roll. Dad came up to watch. He drove all the way from Essex and met me at the ground in Chester. We took the bus with all the lads. I picked up some tackle shields too. It was to be a tough game and it was away at their place. Tim Medwell came and said to put him on the bench. This game was immensely important to the team and me. This would set the tone of how we would perform the rest of the season. I had waited ages for this. I remember scoring twice against them before. One try I had scored seconds after a kick off previously when Ben Cromey was captain. We were now playing a different team and we were also in the same shoes as Chester. They would have the upper hand by playing at home and with no long bus journey. The grass was damp it was soft but not boggy. I had a few lads on the bench and Dad watched from the sides with Carla and Amy the physiotherapists. It was 3-3 at half time. Fresher's, Jim Malony and Stu Wright two of the back rowers stood out for their hard work. I ran in an early try to score running 50 odd meters. Always lead from the front I thought. Later, I put a cheeky chip through for Mark Fraser to gather and score. Mark was a big centre a complete idiot and buffoon but a great strong player. I missed the conversion but it was now 13-6 to us. Chester pulled 3 points back with a penalty but I somehow danced away. I fed Sam Thewlis who was playing wing the ball and he raced 30 meters to score. This time I converted and I remember although my kicking had been bad Medders said, "No, No Liam...you take this." Chester made a cross-field kick. The winger gathered and scored. We were now only 6 points clear. It was only the hard defence from Salford that kept them at bay from scoring again. The clock was ticking. The whistle blew and we had won. I was so happy for the lads. Callum Stone, a fresher was outstanding at scrum half and Zishan the Asian number 8 played out of his skin.

At the end of the game I was pleased as punch. The first one was over. Mission completed. I was so happy for the lad's hard work. It could have gone either way and although we made some slip ups it was the start and the foundations of what I expected from a team. I probably kicked the ball too much slightly nervous at fly half submitting into no other option. Dad came up to Carla and she related what he said onto me. "Well to see Liam's team win was worth the 400 miles round trip." He said. Lovely words I thought from a Father who I never knew was so proud of me.

Eddie Parkes who played back row/2nd row wrote for the Student Direct paper wrote a report for us to enjoy quoting myself. Apparently I ended the game with *"I thought all the new boys did really well. I am proud of the team as a whole. There is obviously a lot of work to be done, but this is the start to the season we wanted"*. We travelled back to Salford University by bus and Dad started his long journey home down south. The 2nd team had also won well 19-10.

Back in Manchester, Tim was itching to go out. We were to meet in the Pav at the student bar on the campus of Salford University. I was mentally and physically drained. It had been a long build up with a magical end. My first game over and complete. I could relax a little now and not worry so much. The job was far from done but I was pleased and just needed to be alone for 15 minutes to unwind and gather my thoughts. It was quite emotional. Tim agreed and left me to be for a bit seeing I was shattered in every way. I did follow shortly after to meet him and the team in the student bar where we partied all night in Manchester at some dodgy student night suited and booted in our number 1s.

Our next game was against Keele. We were confident from winning the week before. I made a break early on in the game but was held up short. It was an exciting match and 0-0 at half time did not reflect the action that had taken places 40 minutes prior. In the second half we had the wind and the slope in our favour but we just did not capitalise and we didn't execute enough with our opportunities. Their hooker scored from a lineout and our heads went down. The winger went over to score too, to make it 10-0. We bounced back and Mark Fraser fed Medders aka Timmy Blanco the ball to score. However the referee deemed it forward. The final whistle went and we had run out of time. I was mortified, embarrassed and clearly upset for my team. In the match report I had said that *"**We are clearly all gutted that we had lost a game that perhaps we should have won. We will regroup on Monday and come out fighting again for the next game.**"*

We went on to beat Manchester Metropolitan weeks later. They were our local rivals and it was nice to stick one on them. To inspire my team I told the lads that their captain had txt me the night before saying they were confident that they were going to beat us in a way that is would ruffle my feathers and put me off. I wanted the lads to react in a way where they wouldn't take a backwards step to cockiness. I wanted them to realise that no team respected us. I wanted them to man up and be counted, to earn respect. They knew I was lying of course but it seemed to work as we finished winning 17-11. It was another away win, this time at Broughton Park, Manchester Metropolitan's ground the other side of the city. My mate Medders aka Timmy Blanco scored the first try but Man Met kicked two penalties to make the score 6-5. Things went from bad to worse as Stu Wright left the field with a shoulder injury. They then scored in the corner from a good move from the number 8 and some woeful defence on our behalf. Callum Stone got the try we needed right before half time when he went over to score in the corner. Bernie our coach gave us an ever-inspirational half time team talk. Sam Thewlis made a break through to beat everyone except the full back but chipped over the top. I raced through to collect the ball and scored under the posts. I converted and the time ran out for

Man Met. Bernie said afterwards *"We would have been bitterly disappointed today if we hadn't have won. It was grit and determination from the whole team that won us the match. Well done everyone"*

We lost at home to UCLAN, University of Central Lancashire 8-0. We were completely outplayed all over the park except the score line didn't suggest this. "Planty" our hooker was sent to the sin bin. A rather emotional volatile character, he was obviously upset. I made a break through and popped the ball to Mark Fraser who was stopped meters from the line with a great tackle from their full back. Bernie told us that conceding 8 points was not a bad thing; it was scoring none that was worrying. I was indeed worried. Losing at home was bad. This was the second time this had happened to us and I started to worry about my decisions as captain and as a fly half.

Our next game was up against Bangor. We needed to bounce back from last week's disappointment and loss. Bangor started well and put us on the back foot with good forward play. It did not last for long and winger Phil White scored the first points of the day. Phil was fast and fairly strong. I had played him inside centre our first game but it was evident that he was more of a winger. The Bangor forwards had self destructed with a forward's play that went wrong and Phil pounced on the ball to score. Max Everest a huge tall prop from Cumbria played his heart out. He also scored and Jody Gregg dropped an audacious goal as well. We took our feet off the gas and started to crumble slightly. We gave away cheap penalties but Bangor were unable to capitalize and only converted one of them. Mark Fraser and Callum Stone scored to make it 23-3 at half time. Callum then scored again in the corner and Ben Cromey who I had handed the kicking duties too converted to make it 30-3. More tries came from myself, Jody and Mark and a third from Callum to make it his hat trick. We won convincingly as Ben Cromey converted all tries to make the score 58-3. I had played in games like that where I was on the receiving end of a thumping. Not a nice feeling and Bangor wanted nothing more than the game to end and I didn't blame them. I played at full back and I was delighted with the team. I thought everyone played well. Our discipline wasn't great at times in the first half but we picked ourselves up and played some good rugby. Hopefully this would give us enough confidence to play Edge Hill next.

So after the Christmas break we regrouped. The game against Edge Hill had been rescheduled. Due to exams we fielded a weak side. However, Matt Norman and Jamie Davis were to make their debuts. We went down 12-0 and at half time we were in a spot of bother and looked like we were in a bit of trouble. I gave a usual half time team talk and things looked on the up after the kick off with the boys playing some good rugby. However, Mark Fraser and I collided causing my ankle to split and I received a deep cut. I hadn't noticed but it was over an inch long in the shape of an L. It stung a bit and I looked down and my thick rugby sock was covered in a small area of dark blood. I had a look and saw the damage. There was a flap of skin and you could almost see the bone. Carla the physio said I needed at least 5-6 stitches. I snapped and said I didn't have time for that. I ordered her to wrap it up in a bandage and tape. I would play on regardless. I wasn't in that much pain it was just flesh that could be sorted later. But lets just say it wasn't life threatening so I played on. I had a rugby team to lead and a match to win. This game was crucial if we wanted to finish top half of the table. I came back on the field as it was regarded as a blood injury. Only then I set Mark up for a try for him to score in the corner. Ben Cromey expertly converted. We put more pressure on them and played a lot of rugby in their half, only to not capitalise. Then bounced back and scored in the corner. Despite Ben Cromey slotting two penalties over the uprights the score ended 19-13. It was another disappointment losing to a good team. We had dug deep but it was with the help of Ben

Cromey who perhaps should not have been playing, as he was not attending University, that made the score line look better. It just went to show how important he was as a key player especially with his kicking abilities to keep us in the game. We were now mid table with three wins and three losses.

I would update the lads accordingly via txt and emails. Sometimes it was like running a kindergarten. Key players would miss training on Monday's our only training session of the week. Some could not play due to work placement and exams etc the usual "Sorry Trig I can't make training as I have to study" excuse was used a lot.

In January 2005 we would come back from our Christmas holiday and I would write to the boys an update. It was key to keep players interested and involved as we still had a few games left to play in the league. A typical email was like this.

"Afternoon gentlemen, welcome back to Salford. Hope the ladies are all treating you well. Just a New Years update.

1. Good luck with exams.
2. Training starts Mon 17th Jan. First games are 2 weeks from then so we only have this session Mon 31st and Monday 2nd. It will just be a bit of touch rugby next Monday just to get into the swing of things, as numbers will be short due to exams and revision.
Proper training begins 24th Jan with Bernie present. (Individual cardio, weight training and even plyometrics if anyone thinks they can keep up with me) are to be done in your own time. When you aren't working out your opponent is and sooner or later you will have to face him!!!!!!!
2nd Feb will be 1st team home against Man Met (Crewe & Alsager), 2nd Team home against Bolton Institute.
The University has won website of the month which has got us the following coverage from the RFU

www.rfu.com/clubs/salforduni and funding within the next few months from the Development plan that was issued by the Committee members (me and Ben Eagles actually) in December. (Money for Kit, tackle suits, balls etc)

3. Now that everyone has been given their student loans please don't blow it on hookers or babysham (as much as I would like to as well) we have tour to pay for. The money needs to be paid asap to Ben Egleneck his number is 07*********.

4. Money from selling the naked calendars also needs to be handed in to Ben. There's no point us setting up a venture to aid tour stash (polo shirts and kit) if people don't hand that cash in. No excuses please.

5. There is a 10s tournament on 16th and 23rd Feb. The first date is for players who have been selected for 2nd team games but maybe haven't had much game time as a sub and for players who haven't played or been selected yet. The week after is an elite side. Mostly 1st team players. By no circumstances do the RFU want 1st team players that will be playing the week after playing on 16th. A registration will be taken, policing this scenario. However 1st and 2nd team players are needed to be present on the Wed 16th to support their teammates like wise the week after. This is a good opportunity for some 2nd team players to get into the elite side and show they have potential.

6. Enjoy the rest of the year academically and more important as a Rugby Club. Lets look forward to some silverware either in the leagues, 10s tournament and on tour in Spain.

Over and out!!!

Luv Liam "Trigger", El Capitan

Around the springtime I got into an argument with a lad in the 24-hour computer room. I had originally tried to help him as the computer he wanted wasn't working. He rejected my help quite arrogantly. I was with Ben Cromey at the time watching rugby clips online. Ben suggested we wind him up a bit and tell him the computer now worked. I cheekily turned round and commenced. He jumped out of his chair started yelling and shouting accusing me of picking on him. He then went to security and they asked for my ID. A few weeks later I got a call from the police. They asked me to come in and talk with them about the incident as he had filed a racial complaint against me. Apparently some eyewitnesses said I had made a comment but others said he had been a complete lunatic and blown my sarcastic remarks out of proportion. I had tried to defuse the situation when he asked "Maybe you don't like me because of my colour?" to which I replied, "listen mate, best you sit down you are giving (and I wont say) a bad name. Be quiet or I will rip that comical beard off you" I went to the police station dressed in a suit and University rugby club tie. I explained my side of the story. I was not sure if the cops were trying to lure me into saying something I should not. I told them that I was the captain of the University rugby team. It was me that picked the side. I told them that I had a Muslim number 8 and a Jewish prop on my side. I was Catholic and I had a Protestant centre. How could I be racist? The CPS dropped all the charges and the case was thrown in the bin.

I can't remember which game it was but on one occasion early in the morning I went down to the fields before the game. It was raining miserably but I went to the pitch before the game to practice goal kicking with Dave Jacobs who was known as Essex Dave. I think I missed 9 out of 10 kicks as Dave watched each one sail the wrong side of the posts without saying a word to me.

We played Crewe and Alsager and Ben Cromey got us off to a good start with a classic drop goal putting three early points on the board. Mark Fraser and Matt Lindsey in the centres made a play and I was able to race over the line to score. Ben Cromey converted as usual and the score was now 10-0. Another penalty by Ben meant it was 13-0 but like always we took our feet off the gas, slipped up and got complacent. We let in two tries and it was now 13-12. We held on for dear life and the game was finally over. Our last game was away against St Martins. It was a complete disaster. Due to exams 5 players could not make it. Catty's 2nd team players were called up as their game had been cancelled. We arrived late too which didn't help. We lost the game 36-0 my last as captain. I gave my final team talk at the end of the match documented by Eddy and it was reported in the Student Direct newspaper. I had said, ***"After losing ten first team players from last season, this year was always going to be tough. The players that have stepped in have played out of their skin. I've been proud to lead the team and the players this season so thank you for that".*** We had won 4 and lost 4 finishing 3rd place in the league. Bernie was pleased with what we had achieved and said under the circumstances of ten 1st team players leaving we had done well as it takes a few years to rebuild any squad. My job was done. We had our AGM and Eddy was finally elected as captain so I handed the job over to him. Did I make a good captain? Who knows? I tried my hardest to do well for the team and lead by example especially when it came to training and commitment. I knew my weaknesses but I did try and work hard on them especially the kicking aspect of my game.

After I was given my final mucky pint in the Pav where a whip round had come to around £18 and they put whatever they could afford from the whip in a pint glass. I didn't throw up but it was pretty bad. Bernie the coach told me to be careful on the night out. The reason they are called Mucky pints was because the Guinness and Baileys would curdle with the lime. It almost looked like solid bits of floating cheese. Mixed together was vodka, Aftershock, Baileys Guinness, red wine, limejuice and Tabasco sauce etc. No one in the history of my playing days has ever enjoyed drinking a mucky pint. I remember Bernie propping up the bar saying "Liam, you are going to pass out asleep in 30 minutes" I lasted the whole night and I think my highlight was seeing Duffy projectile vomit over Eddy in a cab whilst we were on our way out to Manchester. We all ended up in Piccadilly 21's notorious student night. It didn't matter that it had been Eddy but it was bloody funny. I had never seen Duffy in this drunken way before. I think I may have told him to give Eddy the money for the dry cleaning of his suit.

During this period of playing for Salford University and Manchester rugby club I was playing five days a week. A great memory and I loved it. It almost felt like a full time job, like a professional player. Training at Salford was on Mondays; Tuesday's training was at Manchester RFC, University match days were on Wednesdays, training was at Manchester RFC Thursdays, a rest day on Fridays and a game for Manchester RFC on Saturdays. My washing loads were pretty big and I would take it in to work at the bar who let me use the work washing and drying facilities for free.

That spring of 2005, even though I had revision and a dissertation to work on, we would go to Spain again for our tour. This time we were to go to Lloret del Mar. Tim Medwell didn't make it this time. It wasn't the same without him. There would be no street rugby or working at local nightclubs. But I had made friends with a few of the rugby league players. I had previously that academic year, played for them on the wing and we went up to Hull. I came on as a sub and I scored on my debut. They were a good bunch mostly northerners coached by John Blackburn a Salford Reds rugby league development coach. I stayed with a lad called Johnny a short stocky guy. I just needed to pay for my flight although the student University sports girl was a bit annoyed with me and got the needle as I was breaking all the rules, apparently. I arrived late on in the evening. As I had travelled on my own, my cab cost me well over 50 Euros from the airport. I had flown myself rather than take the 30-hour bus through France and Spain. This might have been a better option as I would have had some banter with the lads and perhaps bonded more. I arrived to a sea of carnage of students all in fancy dress. My tour name was simple "W"...that's what I apparently asked the guys to bring home each game...a "Win" and nothing less. Apparently, I once said in a team talk "The beer and pussy always taste better after a W lads!" We played a tournament against other Universities like we had done the year before and I was still captain although it seemed Chris Tyson had taken charge. We did ok but no one really took it seriously. By now most of the team had their cliques. There were the fresher's who were clueless and constantly drunk and then the second team clique of Eddie Parkes, Catty, Porty and Egelneck. None of my real mates were there but I had a laugh all the same.

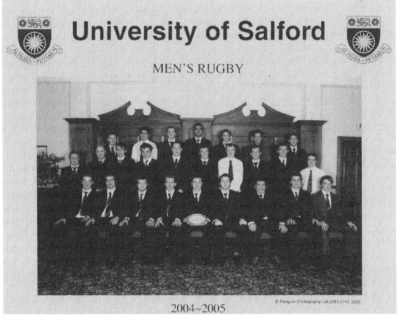

Figure 9 Captaining the University of Salford, Manchester 2004-5

Figure 10 Tim Medwell and me on a post match University rugby social 2005

Chapter 19

Around the time I split my ankle in the spring game while playing for University, I started playing down at Wilmslow RFC. Tim had been playing there and he was now quite settled at fullback/wing for the 1st team. He enticed me down and would give me a lift. As I got to know the lads, Dan Hargreaves the scrum half would also pick me up from Wilmslow station in the evening or Tim would meet me to take us both down there. It was a nice club. A lot smaller than Manchester RFC in a lower league but I enjoyed it. Each week there was a match program and I would be pretty chuffed to see my name in the team line up, something I had not experienced before. I would send them to my Dad back in Essex to read. The coach was called Manny. I watched from the bench that weekend with Tim's dad. Tim, as a care worker was allowed to play rugby as long as his patient or "dude" as he called them, was being supervised by someone who was also qualified. His dad was the perfect bill. Apparently this lad Steve was better behaved then myself as we sat in the stands at Pownell Park. I started to play for the first team. I wasn't really sure I liked Jed an old school hooker who was a bit of a bully in my opinion. Still the old school back room committee members were nice and the club had a good vibe. There was always a bottle of Jameson's flowing around one way and a bottle of Port going around the other, usually bought and instigated by Andy Vasell a big northern prop and a fun guy. I would usually sink a few pints. Stiff and slightly pickled I would venture into Manchester to work at Lime bar on the bar until 3 am. One evening there was a bit of a party. "Johnners" was on the drums and Kerry on the bass. I wanted to play the guitar. I got up, requesting to play and gave a little rendition of Johnny be Goode, the blues song by Chuck Berry. None of the lads knew I played. I wasn't even that good but I started playing and everyone seemed to stop and listen. I shyly looked up from concentrating on the notes I was playing and to my amazement everyone was looking at me slightly shocked. It was a pretty fun night to be fair. We played in South Lancs/Cheshire League one. We played against teams like Leigh, Warrington, Wirral, Northwich, Sanbach, Nutsford and Broughton Park. We also got to play against a team called Vagabonds in the Isle on Man. This meant a nice little road trip away to their place where we would fly into Douglas on a dodgy propeller plane.

My first game for Wilmslow was against Wirrel. I think I came on as a sub. One of the players gave me an absolute shoeing and I had three large stud marks raked down my face from one of their kind forwards. I never knew if it was because I had been a southerner or because I just didn't release the ball. Either way it made me look a bit of a brawler and I got one or two strange looks the next week from girls around campus.

I had never been to the Isle of Man and was rather excited. The flight over was rather loud and bumpy due to the weather and I'm not sure how safe I felt being flown in a propeller plane. But I was excited and I had the weekend off work. Better still it was all paid for out of our subs and union money. I'm not sure if I paid subs that year being a poor student. Iain Tyson was in the zone and chatted up a fine female on the plane. Great charm and tight lyrics had Tyson. He was a good tackler of the game too. A good full back not that quick or nimble though. He always carried a bit of timber but was a solid defender. Tim Medwell had not been picked. It was a massive surprise to me and everyone else. He was absolutely fuming by the decision and found out in the changing rooms one evening. I felt bad as he had been talking about this tour for a while and we were both excited to go away and play.

The rugby pitch was right next to the Moto GP track and also very windy being near the seafront, which happened to be the blustery Irish Sea. I played pretty well and scored a brace of tries finally on a fast ground pitch. We ended up winning 41-13.

Tyson got man of the match and we all went out and got completely smashed. Phil Carr and I teamed up and went solo for a bit drinking in this pub full of mongs who looked slightly inbred. Bob our talented fly half managed to drop his phone down the drain. Our hotel had a nightclub at the bottom and we managed to get back there to party. As residents we got in for free. We had won the game and partied until the early hours of the morning. Owen Fergus and I had gone off with two girls to a party. I passed out. We then had to do the "Walk of Shame" in the morning back to our hotel. Very hung over we hurried back in case the bus to the airport left without us. Then we flew back to Manchester where I said goodbye to the Wilmslow lads. I trekked back to my student dorm in Salford.

We would play our last game of season 2004-5 away at Broughton Park. We never really got out of first gear and we were always on the back foot. Dad drove up from London with Ann to watch. Medders and Tyson watched from the sideline. The ground was fairly nice with a great clubhouse, balcony and seating for spectators. Corina, a girl I was seeing at the time came down to watch as well. We lost the game badly and didn't make the play off's which was a big shame. But that was rugby and how we performed on the day determined our fate.

Dan Hargreaves the scrum half worked for Pinsent Masons solicitors and organised some 7s jerseys to be made. My tour name would be "Del Boy" after the cockney character from the comedy show "Only Fools and Horses". We were warned about a ringer playing for Leigh who was playing full time at Rotherham RFC. Tim and I managed to smash him early on in the game. However, as we tired towards the end of the game we allowed him that half-yard extra. This was too much for him and he would race away to the try line laughing at us. We later learned it was a guy called Dave Strettle who went on to play for Harlequins RFC and Saracens RFC and also England. I was sin binned in one game for retaliation. I threw a punch and that was the end of my tournament. The tour shirt was a nice souvenir, at least and I still have mine today. That summer I would graduate and finally earned myself a 2.1 honours degree. I continued to play for Wilmslow RFC and became a regular first team player. The following season I was much more involved. I remember playing at a game in Hoylake, Cheshire. Tim was back playing at his usual fullback position and me on the right wing. Tim drifted out wide and took the man with him opening up a massive gap for me where the defence hadn't drifted across. I spotted the opportunity and called a switch running 30 odd meters to go in and score. Bob converted and the score was 7-3. Tim said he had seen the smile on my face. I guess I had got slightly excited before scoring. Tim and I had been out the night before extremely naughty of course and I felt terrible on the drive home with him and Will Masters. We ended up winning 12-10. Tim also scored. I returned the favour this time and set him up. The back line worked its magic once more, and I moved inside to straighten the line and Tim at full back touched down out wide. However, a lot of games I seemed to struggle. Each week players like Alex McLennan a big lanky second row and old school would tell me to back myself and go for it. I just wanted early ball. If the ball did make it to me past Kiwi or Ross I seemed to only get it one on one with the opposite winger and I had about 5 meters to the touchline to use.

In the November in 2005 I had some trouble at work feeling the pressure I walked out and quit my job in the bar. I ended up getting drunk at the Manchester bars letting off some steam. I didn't make the game the next day against Leigh. I made up some excuse that I had been ill but Tim knew I was lying and probably so did the coaches. Luckily they went onto win 19-14 with the replacement winger scoring. My absence was mentioned in the Manchester Evening News. The next week at training the 2nd team captain Waggy came up to me and grabbed me. He wanted to kill me. Because I had let the team down they were a winger short, one of the 2nd team wingers was called up to duty. "Waggy" was clearly annoyed as he now had lost a player and decided to take it out on me by taking the law into his our hands. Pretty harsh I thought for a thirty something has been and crap player, to start on a young graduate. That week Steve Swindells, the backs coach took me aside in the dressing room. Everyone had gone out onto the pitch right before the whistle. He told me a few people had doubted me to play but he had vouched for me despite what had happened the week before. He said that I was the best winger of the club and to go out and show everyone what I could do. I liked Steve. He had a wonky nose like me. But apart from that, that's where our similarities ended. He was a northerner and I was a southerner. He could kick the ball and I couldn't and he had played at England under 21's level. Apparently in 1999/2000 he had the best kicking ratio and points scored in league rugby, higher than even Johnny Wilkinson in the Premiership.

Just before Christmas of 2005 Wilmslow RFC flew over again to Isle of Man. This time Tim Medwell my mate and rugby guru would make the trip. However, it was a tight game and our defence gave way in a comedy last minute error. We reviewed the tape and in my opinion you could have blamed Ben Day or myself. However Tim Medwell, just gave up sulking and put his hands on his hips in disgust at our defensive error, another one of his classic miss tackles.

At the end of Jan 2006 the Salford Boys had some bad news. I was still in Manchester. Eddy was captaining the team and I received a telephone call. Stu Wright, one of the fresher's from my team, had tragically died. He was now a 2nd year student. Apparently he had diabetes and slipped into a coma either with too much insulin or not enough. It shocked us all. I then moved to London but I came up a few weeks later. A memorial game was played and I was asked to come up and play. I arrived to the wet Castle Irwell pitches slightly late. There was a group of maybe 70 people all in a circle for a minute's silence in honour of Stu's tragic death. Stu had given me a CD with lots of rugby pictures on for the University rugby website I was building at the time and in charge of. I had accused Stu of giving me the CD with a virus on it. In fact I had deleted some pictures from the website server and thought the worst about Stu's CD he had given me. I called him ranting on about it etc. We played together since that and he made some wonderful runs, as he hit inch perfect lines off me breaking through the gaps. I would txt him and praise him. Eddy had asked me to get other people on board as he was short of players and Stu came to mind. I didn't make his funeral sadly although I am glad we made up our differences before it was too late. It hurt a few of the lads and Stu's ex girlfriend Kat too. We had wanted to donate a park bench for spectators to be able to sit on down by the rugby fields but his family declined. That would be my last game for Salford University. I think I wracked up around 22 tries in 34 matches over a course of 6 years.

In Feb 2006, I would move down to London after I secured my first job in the field of television. I was at Tim's house in Macclesfield the day I got offered the position and he high fived me while I was on the phone to the lady in the human resources office in London. Wilmslow would pay for my train fare for me to come back up and play. Seeing as we neared promotion and I had been there most of the season they suggested that when I had a weekend off to do so. There were other wingers at the club but for some reason they believed in me and thought it fair considering I had been there since pre season. That April 2006 our last game of the league was against Anselmians who came close to winning. In the words of the Manchester Evening News *"Flying winger Liam Dunseath's rescue act was memorable. With three men powering for the line, his heroic last-ditch tackle not only saved a certain try, but wrapped up the ball to prevent the off-load".* We ended up winning 29-17 and this secured our play off game against St Benedict's.

On May 3rd 2006, we entertained the visitors for the last game. I had scored a handful of tries with Wilmslow but I had never scored at home surprisingly. A demon I thought needed to be exercised and this was the day. Tries came from Tim Medwell, Chris Jones, Will Masters, Steve Braddock, Mark Walmsley and Jamie Fletcher. I too managed to get on the scoreboard. I received the ball at first receiver and managed to just get on the outside of my man to go over and score. It was a proud moment to have finally scored at home at Pownall Park in front of so many friends. With our seven-try demolition of the Cumbrian side St Benedict's, we had clinched promotion to North Two West. As the whistle went, the champagne bottles were ready and we celebrated long into the night. That would be my last game for Wilmslow 1st team but I've been back a few times to the club. In Oct 2009 was the 100th birthday of the club. I went up for a bit of a reunion and I partied hard that night with Tyson, Medders and co. Up until this season 2012/13, Tyson and Medders have been playing 2nd team. None of the 2005 team remained in the 1st team, perhaps except Bob and his trusty boot. Tim has retired after too many monstrous tackles...I don't think so... and Tyson for being too old. Steve Peters and Steve Swindells the coaches have moved on, as have various other players. But the usual suspects Barry Fisher, Grant and Keith the barman are still there today all about to check in to old peoples homes.

We had won our last game in The Powergen Cup and would travel down to Luton RFC in the next round. I had played there around 1995/6 with my club Upper Clapton at colt level. Tim and I travelled down the night before to get an early night. The club was right next to the M1. They had a nice clubhouse and good pitch. Dad and Ann came to watch. From the off they set the standard and showed us how well organised and drilled they were. I wasn't intimidated though. I was now playing against some southerners and I wasn't taking a backwards step in what I thought to be also my own backyard. We let in some early tries then pulled a few back. I only really remember charging down a conversion, in fact it was the only one I have ever done. I was pretty chuffed as we were losing badly and I wanted to show the lads I hadn't given up. However, we lost the game and we were now knocked out of the cup. I remember thinking that although Luton RFC were in Bedford League one, I didn't see the other wingers or backline as better than me. Maybe we lost too many line outs and other set pieces which would mean that their forwards were superior to ours. For whatever the reason we didn't win. I had declined a job interview and remember telling the lady who had called me from human resources that I was playing in the Powergen cup 4th round. To me it was a big deal. Unfortunately they never called me back and asked me what other day might be convenient. I was not too bothered. I always loved the chance to play rugby.

Figure 11 Powering towards the line

Figure 12 On the attack @ Wilmslow 2006

Figure 13 Wilmslow RFC wins Promotion 2006

Chapter 20

I asked Steve Swindells our backline coach what I should do once back down south. I asked him about Richmond RFC and he said I should have a go. They were in London League one, at the time almost equivalent to Luton who had been in Bedford League one. Richmond used to be quite a famous club with several international players such as Argentinean Agustín Pichot, England flying winging Dan Luger, hooker Brian Moore, and Welsh Scott Quinell who I now am lucky to work with. I went down there towards the end of the season. We trained on Tuesdays and Thursdays. I hadn't been there since 1995 when I had played with Upper Clapton the day we beat Ruislip RFC and won the Middlesex Cup. In Feb 2006, I started working at SIS Racing channel and that summer I started pre-season training with Richmond RFC. It started in late June. I remember thinking that was a bit early. There were a lot of players there. It was up by the duel carriageway of Richmond near the famous Sun Inn pub. They had two coaches for the backs. A couple of Welsh blokes both called Steve. Small guys but they both knew their onions if you know what I mean. Most Welsh lads who have been involved in rugby usually are pretty slick and even though these lads were mid forties they definitely would have once played at a good standard. The Director of Rugby was a guy called Brett Taylor. He had been the USA National Coach and had taken them to the World Cup in 2003. I thought this was a great achievement. He reminded me a bit like Tony Blair in the way he portrayed what he was trying to say. He wasn't a tough looking hard guy and didn't need to curse or swear but he seemed to speak intelligently, especially about the game and the clubs ethos in playing. He would explain in depth ways of coaching why passes went to the floor because of how the elbow had come up too high and where the hands had followed through too. The drills we did and basic moves were filtered through each team and each player would rotate into different positions, so they understood it thoroughly. I started to catch the eye of some of the 1st team players and coaches. I felt confident, other players would make small conversation but it did seem like a friendly club. I was fit from playing at Wilmslow and I had started going to the local gym again.

That summer though with my shift patterns at work it was tough. I was trying to leave work on time but it was not easy to get from Old Street in the city to Richmond on the District and Northern line via Embankment. Sometimes, on the District line there would be a lot of delays especially if it was wet and a wash out due to heavy rain. Luckily in July 2006 I moved to in between Ravenscourt Park, Shepherds Bush and Acton with my University friend Simon Burgees. To get back from training at Richmond would only take about 30 minutes compared to the two hours to get back to Epping. If I hadn't eaten I would get back after 11 pm and then up again at 6 am to leave for work that started at 8 am. So it wasn't ideal for me.

A week before my first game during training I took on a prop. Not the best thing to do when you receive the ball from a static position. It was a tackling defensive session. I got munched and hurt my shoulder pretty bad. I knew there was an issue so I stopped. The swelling started instantly and I was forced to ice it all week at work. The chef at the canteen at work would give me a huge frozen bloke of pastry. That way it would mould into the shape of my shoulder helping the injured swelling decrease. It bruised up pretty bad but I was free to play in the trial game. We would play a game of a mixture of 1st and 2nd team players. Some 1st team players would not even play, as the coaches already knew their skills. I felt like I did well. I made sure that Neil Piggot the cocky fullback knew who I was. People were calling me his nemesis. He couldn't get round me or pass me even though he was bloody quick and extremely deceptive. He was a posh bastard clearly a public school boy and I had to work hard to track him. I seemed to look good and sharp and enjoyed the day. It was enough to get me into the 2nd team and I made what was called the 50 elite gold squad. I was given some free stash. Everyone likes free kit but I remember being hassled for the subs that were around £100. I was only making £1150 a month at the time and this seemed quite a lot. Most of the other lads had good jobs in the city. The 1st team captain drove a BMW Z3. I mean this was Richmond we were talking about.

I played at Richmond that autumn and spring for the 2nd team and I was scoring a few tries. Andy Molloy was a big strong ginger centre. It was good playing around him, as he was a well-drilled slick player. One game I turned round whilst in a huddle and said "Come on lads lets show these Ealing wankers that we are not just a load of posh Richmond cunts!" To which one player responded and said, "Well you certainly aren't" We would play teams such as Barking, London Scottish, Barnes, and Blackheath. We had a good side though. We had some big forwards with a fast backline. I was playing wing/fullback and was making good use of the ball and the fast ground pitches.

The next season I did exactly the same. I trained hard for pre season. I was now working at Setanta Golf channel, which meant I would play on Saturdays and then go to work around 5 pm to start the television show for 8 pm. After one game though I got dropped to the third team after I refused to fill up the water bottles for the 2nd team. The clubhouse was miles away from the fields and I told Pecky I was in charge of the kicking tee (as I was a sub) and to ask someone else to go. Looking back it was a bit of a pathetic excuse but then so was my punishment. Pecky the young coach said I wasn't good enough anymore and I was told that first team players had been appalled at my behaviour for not wanting to help out. It was a bit much and I was going to apologies to the whole training session of 50 players sarcastically but I thought best not to. So as the season went on I was to train with the third team each Tuesday and Thursday. Medders, who was up north, laughed at me. He thought it was quite funny that I was playing in such a low ranked side. My goal had been to get into the 1st team and to score tries there. I would look over at the 2nd team players and feel like I had said goodbye to my friends. Andy Molloy, Elvis and Cameron had been my mates and we had a laugh together.

That autumn of 2007 was the Rugby World Cup in France. I managed to get some tickets for the England v Tonga game. My cousins Gian Paolo and his son Lorenzo lived in Paris and I secured some tickets for the game at Parc de Prance, a French national stadium. I had been around 1994 to watch Paris Saint German play Lens and Gian Paolo had taken me as a treat. It was my turn to repay the favour as an adult. England won convincingly and I saw Paul Sackey score two great tries, one of which he ran the length of the field. Epi Taione who Tim had played against when he was at Sale RFC academy was playing for Tongan at centre. It was nice to have three generations of cousins at the game and I brain washed my half French, half Italian cousin Lorenzo to support "Le Rose".

Figure 14 Three generations of cousins England v Tonga, Paris 2007

Around the same time, one night in October 2007, I hit a tackle shield during training. I felt something painful happen. I had never experienced this before. I had had a few stingers where the nerve in your neck is temporarily jarred and gets pinched sending a shock down your arm but this was different. It felt like lightning had zapped me. I took myself off from the training session and went to see the physio although they said nothing was wrong with me. I went to see my local doctor days later. My index finger and thumb remained numb. The weather began to get cold and I noticed it more on colder days. Also, on the train when I was sat down and my arms were tight by my sides (if it was busy) I would begin to feel uncomfortable and numbness occurring. I managed to get an MRI appointment through my doctor on Boxing Day. Finally the surgeon told me in the February 2008 that between the vertebrae of C4-5 in my neck, the nerve than ran down my arm to my index finger and thumb was being pinched. This was causing the numbness and pain. I stopped training, as it was painful to throw a ball just a few yards. Even in the spring of 2008, a month after my MRI result, I found it hard to throw a ball when I went over for spring break and trained with the Daytona rugby guys. Carlos however leant me his traction device. It works by pulling your neck out. You clamp your head in the vice and pump slowly. I would also have physical therapy free on the NHS once a week that helped ease the area. It would help when I clicked my neck and tension would be released with a loud clicking noise, probably discouraged by medics. I'm sure my posture didn't help me but within time my neck started to feel better. I could run and move my arms without pain or stiffness.

In the April of 2008 I would start playing Rugby League for Hainault Bulldogs. I was indeed worried about my neck. The fitness training was hard but fun. The coach was a huge fat guy Kevin from up north. He was my kind of guy. In your face, direct, upfront and always taking the piss. He was from Leeds to be exact. The players were a mixture of rugby league players and rugby union and we trained at Barking RFC way out east on the District line. It was indeed far from where I lived but it started to give me confidence to play again. My first game would be against Eastern Rhinos based out in Colchester Essex. The first minute of the game and my first tackle...boom! My head was split. It was just a small gash but the blood trickled out as head wounds always do. Luckily it wasn't too bad and I went on to score. Each game my confidence grew and grew and I enjoyed running in a few tries for the 2nd team. I was called up to play 1st team as a sub and after I had made a couple of appalling passes and a knock on we found ourselves camped on our own try line. The ball was spun wide. I had seen the passer wind up a long pass and shot up out of the defensive line. I made sure the receiver got smashed. I hit him right under the rib cage and dumped him on the ground. I had buried him into next week and the guys on the sideline made me aware of their appreciation as this not only saved us a certain try but turned the ball over for us to get out of danger. To whoever reads this you may find this weird but I used an unconventional way to psych myself up before a game. I would tell myself on the train that tomorrow I would be dead and that today was my last day of my life so I must leave with being remembered for something. Very weird I know but I wanted people to say, if it did happen "wow only yesterday he scored two amazing tries and tackled his heart out". It worked a few times. I'm a firm believer in tapping into the mind to help in sport but its what ever works for you I suppose.

That June I would go over to the USA and start my epic South Finals and Nationals adventure previously explained. I really enjoyed the rugby league. It was a different game to what I was used to. I enjoyed having 10 extra meters to work in once you had the ball. It was tough work defending though. Just like rugby union, a player has to constantly talk and communicate with his teammates, constantly be aware of the holes around him and keep a defensive shape tight whilst retreating backwards. It's a game where you can't go missing. I enjoyed reading the articles each week in the Ilford Recorder newspaper that I'd present my Dad. I didn't socialise much although we did have a good knees up in an Irish Pub in Seven Kings at the end of the season.

In September 2010 I was invited to work in India for the Commonwealth Games, essentially for the BBC. It was for the host broadcaster and I went out for 15 days to Delhi. I was involved filming the marathon, road races and cycling. I had ignored all the negatives that were in the press at the time about Delhi and the organisation of the games. I wanted to see for myself a whole new world. Luckily, I had two days off and I would go to the Delhi University where the rugby 7s was being held. I used my TV security pass to get in. Although I wanted to sit with the locals and experience some Indian culture, I was told I was not allowed. The temporary seating had no cover and to be honest I would have fried in the 44 degree heat (111 degrees Celsius). I ended up sneaking into the players lounge in the stadium for a "Liam Buffet" pretending to know what I was doing and that I may have been somewhat important. Later I would meet Laurence Dallaglio as well as the Indian 7s team. Some of their friends insisted on taking me out later that night. I did indeed take them up on their offer and I asked my driver Praveen to take me to Connaught Place in Delhi. He was too shy to come in perhaps due to the Caste system in India he knew his place. The lads bought beer and sung songs. I challenged one guy to a drinking contest and we downed a few Indian rums. Next, I stupidly suggested a Tabasco contest with Jahangir, one of the players. I must have been drunk, I mean who challenges an Indian man to a spicy competition. I failed miserably. There I was in the middle of Delhi, with Indian rugby lads doing the same as I would have back home in the UK, it was quite bizarre.

Chapter 21

In October 2011, I had worked all spring and all summer. I had a cortisone injection in the spring and my shoulder was feeling better. I had been to a family wedding on the Italian island of Sardinia. I went with Kirsty and we had a lovely time enjoying my cousin's wedding, lovely beaches with some great food and wine. I didn't get a chance to go to the village where my grandmother came from. I also wanted to meet and train with a local rugby team.

Italians aren't renowned for their rugby. We all know how passionate they are about football. They have won some shock games in the Six Nations and made some upsets in the past but I was guessing even with most of their star players playing in Premiership, Magners League and Top 14 French league, the Sardinian rugby would be like the island itself, somewhat slightly backwards to the mainland.

I flew back over in the October. I had written to Oristano RFC via email a month previously. I have been and stayed in Oristano a few times before. It's a nice town, quiet and close to the beach. I thought this would be appropriate as I had cousins in the area, too. I explained in my email that I was English with a Sardinian grandmother. One guy wrote back in English. His name was Andrea and was my main point of contact as was Giovanni the captain and we made friends on Facebook. Andrea was one of the board members of the club. He very kindly arranged and booked a hotel for me in Oristano. Actually it was a hostel that was almost like a hotel. I couldn't tell the difference. I paid for it but they offered to pick me up each night for training. Again this showed how far the rugby brotherhood stretches anywhere you go as well as the local hospitality. I flew to Cagliari and took a train up to Oristano. I met my Mother's cousin Antonietta and her son Nicola for a coffee and some ice cream at their family home near the town station and then she dropped me at the hotel.

That evening, the rugby guys picked me up. It was quite surreal. Andrea spoke perfect English. He was quite funny and sarcastic. He must have learnt that from people he had studied with or English TV shows. We drove maybe fifteen minutes just outside the town to the rugby club. It was as I expected an old clubhouse, a rusting grill outside and a pitch that was bare. Where there was grass it was thick with areas of weeds. There were farms either side growing corn and other arable produce. The evening was warm and the cicadas were loud. I walked into the changing room. All these rough-looking farmer style Sardinian men were all happy to come and introduce themselves. I had many names to quickly learn, lots of hand shaking and repetitive hellos and how are you (bonjourno come stai in Italian).

I booted up unsure what to expect really. I had hoped to help them in some drills for rucking, tackling, defence and attack moves. They had a coach whose name was Peppe. He was a tough-looking, bald, dark man with stubble.

We started to train and I was constantly listening to him. He spoke in Italian. I wanted to learn words quickly like flat and deep, left and right. After a longish warm up jog he put us through several drills. People began lazily and many balls got dropped. Peppe would start shouting at the guys quite angrily. No one answered. I tried to understand maybe I was making mistakes in the drill so listening attentively was critical. I didn't want him to rant at me in Italian for basic errors.

It was nice to be there even on the uneven badly grassed pitch. My cousins came down to watch and to say hello. I was inclined as an Englishman to do well and to train hard. Later they took me out for pizza and a couple of Sardinian beers called Ischnusa. They wouldn't even let me pay. I was their rugby guest and now their friend. Although they all spoke in Italian amongst themselves I was happy being around them. It was very civilized eating at 11.30 pm at night, quite different to most other rugby socials I had been involved in, in the past. I was also happy to leave sober without the horrible rugby hangover the next day. We trained Tuesday, Wednesday and Thursday I went home to the UK on the Friday. One session I had a chance to be physical. I was a bit worried about my shoulder but it held up. I found myself stealing balls at the break down getting to my feet quickly to rob the player before his back up arrived at the breakdown. This was new for me. Players were too quick in the UK to the breakdown and I found it easy.

On my last night it happened to be Andrea's birthday. The lads decided to have a cook out and BBQ grill. It was clear who was the chef in charge. It was a big prop. He would make wild boar sausages and cook steaks on the grill for about twenty of us. Some of the women's team came down. Everyone had a beer or two and smoked cigarettes outside the clubhouse. In fact, it was more of a small, weathered building. It had a kit room, changing rooms with showers and a small storage room. I was very dehydrated after our training session from the running I had done. I hadn't done anything all summer as I had been working so hard. My body had taken a few knocks and I was stiff. But it felt good. Everyone asked when I was coming back but I simply didn't know. It's now a year on and although I've kept in touch, I haven't been back although I'd like to, especially to play. It would be nice to have played with them and have my cousins come and watch what is normally regarded as a non-Italian sport. Before I went back to my hotel after my third training session, all the players signed a rugby ball for me. It was a great little present to take home. Some of them wrote in English which I thought was a nice touch and others wrote in Italian. Words like "A Presto" which means "See you soon!" and "Grazie Liam" one wrote "God Save the Queen" in English. Andrea told me his sister was sick. He told me there was always hope though. I was thinking about that in June 2012 throughout my rugby tour and wondered if it was hope that had always inspired me and pushed me forward with rugby and life. He later in the year sent me his Oristano rugby t-shirt in the post. Another nice gesture of friendship I thought.

In Jan 2012, I started playing for Imperial Medical University, as I knew Craig Nightingale from Rosslyn Park RFC. I played a few games for them against some young fit and well-organised University teams. I was invited to some of the after match celebrations and I witnessed again the young fresher initiations that were worse than mine 12 years previously. One game there was to be too much alcohol flowing I had to get myself home at 11 pm I was so drunk. I let the younger lads take over; I was too old for this kind of debauchery now.

So what's in store for today and looking to the future? Well I'm taking a little time off from training. The summer of 2012 was hard and tired me out. I haven't run or been to the gym in almost three months. I have most Saturdays booked up with work so I can't play. I am generally lucky enough to be at a Premiership game as part of the television crew. I work as an editor along with various pundits making analysis of the game of rugby. If you are ever lucky to watch Sky Sports Rugby you will see my face on the "Frontline." I make the analysis with the telestrator that animates lines, arrows and circles around players. Usually it's with Dean Ryan but sometimes its Pat Sanderson who's also an ex-England player or it might be the legendary Welsh Scott Quinell. I've worked with Dean the most. He won six caps for England; he played for London Wasps winning the Premiership and Coached Gloucester RFC as well as Help for Heroes Northern Hemisphere squad. Dean took the time to do a small video shoot with me in 2011 at Twickenham for the Help the Heroes charity. Not many people are lucky enough to sit next to a guy like him at the office. He's great to work with and always spots important passages of play of attack and defence. He has great banter and I'm always keen to ask him questions about the game and his own playing days. It's been a nice route to go down in terms of learning the game more as well as for my career too. Dean reckons my nose is worse than Mike Tindell's and once when I asked if he ever took a penalty kick he told me that it was his job to give them away, quality lad.

I get to go to many of the stadiums and I go away filming the Amlin and Heineken European cups. I'm still learning now the structure of teams and how the forward plays work, through the work I do of analysis on television. I've considered coaching but it isn't a passion I have right now. I did volunteer to the local Primary school Sacred Heart, Battersea and they embraced me gratefully for taking the after-school rugby club. But right now I do not know enough how to get the best out of players. It's not something I will write off just yet though. I will continue to play the odd game where I can here and there when I have a Saturday off work.

One thing is for sure I have loved the game over the last twenty-one years and writing this book has been a flashback into so many fun memories. Rugby to me is a brotherhood made up of special people. They can be all shapes and sizes and like a chessboard there's a position for everyone. Rugby players can come from all walks of life and all professions. It a game where two teams beat the living daylights out of each other then socialise together in the bar after. I was lucky I had a bit of speed to get away from the danger of being tackled. Real men play rugby and I'm proud to be part of this bunch. Am I an unknown rugger? Those who have played with me would say no. They witnessed the things I did, good and bad on the pitch and off it. The magic I had created. They have shared the good and bad times with me, perhaps in the bigger picture though, in the media and public then, of course, yes. But in my opinion no rugby player is unknown. Someone out there will always remember him, for something decent or magical he did that game. Hopefully one of those someone's that will be remembered will be me.

Special Thanks to Pam Scott & Chris Palmer

Pictures by: -

www.penguinphotography.co.uk

David Barpal www.dcbphotos.com

Dave Stephenson www.numinaphoto.com

www.sportswurlz.com

Paddy Mulchrone paddy@mulchronemedia.com

3868761R00092

Printed in Great Britain
by Amazon.co.uk, Ltd.,
Marston Gate.